# WORLD ENGLISH 2

## Real People • Real Places • Real Language

Kristin L. Johannsen / Rebecca Tarver Chase

HEINLE
CENGAGE Learning

Australia • Brazil • Japan • Korea • Mexico • Singapore • Spain • United Kingdom • United States

**HEINLE**
CENGAGE Learning

**World English 2**
**Real People • Real Places • Real Language**
Kristin L. Johannsen
Rebecca Tarver Chase

Publisher: Jason Mann

Commissioning Editor: Carol Goodwright

Development Editor: Louisa Essenhigh

National Geographic Editorial Liaison:
Leila Hishmeh

Technology Development Manager:
Debie Mirtle

Director of Global Marketing: Ian Martin

Product Manager: Ruth McAleavey

Content Project Editor: Amy Smith

ELT Production Controller: Denise Power

Compositor: MPS Content Services

ISBN: 978-1-1112-1644-3

**Heinle, Cengage Learning**
Cheriton House
North Way
Andover
Hampshire
SP10 5BE
United Kingdom

Cengage Learning is a leading provider of customized learning solutions with office locations around the globe, including Singapore, the United Kingdom, Australia, Mexico, Brazil, and Japan. Locate your local office at:
**international.cengage.com/region**

Cengage Learning products are represented in Canada by Nelson Education, Ltd.

Visit Heinle online at **elt.heinle.com**

Visit our corporate website at **www.cengage.com**

Although every effort has been made to contact copyright holders before publication, this has not always been possible. If notified, the publisher will undertake to rectify any errors or omissions at the earliest opportunity.

Cover Image: Kenneth Garrett/National Geographic Image Collection, Karnak, Egypt

Printed in China
3 4 5 6 7 8 9 10 - 15 14 13 12 11

# CONTENTS

| ✓ Unit Goals | Grammar | Vocabulary | Listening | Speaking and Pronunciation | Reading and Writing |
|---|---|---|---|---|---|
| **Food from the Earth** page 2 | | | | | |
| • Compare what people usually do with what they are doing now<br>• Identify regional staple foods<br>• Talk about traditional family dishes<br>• Understand how a regional food becomes an international dish | Verb tense review:<br>Simple present tense vs. present continuous tense<br>*I **eat** rice every day.*<br>*She**'s cooking** fish now.*<br>Simple past tense (regular and irregular)<br>*We **learned** how to make pizza yesterday.* | Geographical regions<br>Climate<br>Food staples | Focused listening<br>An interview: rice farming | Comparing different regions: discussing their climate and their food<br>Linking sounds: final consonant followed by a vowel | "A Slice of History"<br>Responding to an email |
| **Communication** page 14 | | | | | |
| • Communicate with people from different cultures<br>• Make small talk with new people<br>• Use small talk to *break the ice*<br>• Learn how professionals *break the ice* | Present perfect tense<br>*He **has traveled** to many countries.*<br>Signal words: *already, ever, yet*<br>**Have** you **ever seen** a giraffe? | Culture, communication, and gestures<br>Small talk | Listening for general understanding<br>Conversations: small talk | Talking about what you have or haven't done<br>Making small talk<br>*Have* or *has* vs. contractions | "Taking Pictures of the World"<br>Writing opinions |
| **Cities** page 26 | | | | | |
| • Describe your city or town<br>• Explain what makes a good neighborhood<br>• Discuss an action plan<br>• Make predictions about cities in the future | Future with *will*<br>*The city **will be** cleaner.*<br>*Will* + time clauses<br>*I**'ll** check out the neighborhood **before** I rent an apartment.* | City life<br>Maps | General and focused listening<br>A radio interview: Jardin Nomade in Paris | Discussing good and bad elements in a neighborhood<br>Predicting the future of cities<br>Emphatic stress | "Megacities"<br>Writing a paragraph |
| **The Body** page 38 | | | | | |
| • Discuss ways to stay healthy<br>• Talk about lifestyles<br>• Suggest helpful natural remedies<br>• Understand how germs affect the body | Review of comparatives, superlatives, and equatives<br>*The skin is **the** body's **largest** organ.*<br>Infinitive of purpose<br>*You can drink tea with honey **to help** a sore throat.* | Human organs<br>Parts of the body<br>Everyday ailments | Focused listening<br>A doctor's appointment | Talking about food and ingredients that are good for you<br>Suggesting easy remedies<br>Linking with comparatives and superlatives | "Tiny Invaders"<br>Writing an excuse for a sick child |
| **Challenges** page 50 | | | | | |
| • Talk about facing challenges<br>• Reflect on past accomplishments<br>• Use *too* and *enough* to talk about abilities<br>• Describe a personal challenge | Simple past tense vs. past continuous tense<br>*We **were eating** dinner when you **called**.*<br>*Enough, not enough, too* + adjective<br>*He was **old enough** to sail alone.* | Physical and mental challenges<br>Phrasal verbs | Listening for general understanding<br>An interview: Jenny Daltry, herpetologist | Discussing challenges<br>Talking about abilities<br>Words that end in *–ed* | "Arctic Dreams and Nightmares"<br>Writing a journal entry |
| **Transitions** page 62 | | | | | |
| • Use the simple past tense and past perfect tense to talk about milestones in your life<br>• Talk about the best age to do something in your life<br>• Use *how* questions to get more information<br>• Describe an important transition in your life | Simple past tense vs. present perfect tense<br>*I **lived** alone in 2005.*<br>*I**'ve lived** alone for five years now.*<br>*How* + adjective or adverb<br>**How tall** is he? | Stages of life<br>Adjectives for age: *youthful, childish, mature* | General and focused listening<br>A radio program: healthy tips from an Okinawan centenarian | Talking about something you did<br>Discussing the best age for life transititons<br>ə sound | "Coming of Age the Apache Way"<br>Writing a paragraph to describe a life transition |

| | Unit Goals | Grammar | Vocabulary | Listening | Speaking and Pronunciation | Reading and Writing |
|---|---|---|---|---|---|---|
| **UNIT 7** | **Luxuries page 74**<br>• Explain how we get luxury items<br>• Talk about needs and wants<br>• Discuss what makes people's lives better<br>• Evaluate the way advertising creates desire for products | Present passive voice<br>*Jewelry* **is given** *as a gift.*<br>Passive voice with *by* (present tense)<br>*This blouse* **was made** *by well-paid workers.* | Luxury items<br>Import/export items<br>Past participles of irregular verbs | Focused listening<br>Discussions:<br>the world flower market | Discussing luxuries and necessities<br>Talking about improving your life<br>Sentence stress: content vs. function words | "Perfume: The Essence of Illusion"<br>Writing a magazine ad |
| **UNIT 8** | **Nature page 86**<br>• Use conditionals to talk about real situations<br>• Talk about possible future situations<br>• Describe what animals do<br>• Give your opinion about a problem in nature | Real conditionals in the future<br>*If I* **have** *time tomorrow, I'll call you.*<br>Quantifiers (review)<br>*Raccoons eat* **many** *different kinds of food.* | Nouns and adjectives to describe animals<br>Adverbs of manner | Listening for general understanding and for specific information<br>A radio program: the bluefin tuna | Role-playing to promote environmental action to make oceans sustainable<br>Phrases in sentences | "Return of the Gray Wolf"<br>Writing a paragraph to give an opinion |
| **UNIT 9** | **Life in the Past page 98**<br>• Discuss life in the past<br>• Talk about your grandparents' daily lives<br>• Compare past and present ways of getting things done<br>• Consider the impact of the Columbian Exchange | *Used to/would*<br>*Native Americans* **used to** *make their shoes out of deerskin.*<br>Past passive voice<br>*Igloos* **were built** *with blocks of ice.* | Activities and artifacts<br>Indian innovations<br>Separable phrasal verbs | Focused and general listening<br>An interview: archaeologist's excavation | Discussing daily life in the past based on archaeological discoveries<br>Reduction of *used to* | "The Columbian Exchange"<br>Writing a journal entry of life in an imaginary world |
| **UNIT 10** | **Travel page 110**<br>• Talk about preparations for a trip<br>• Talk about different kinds of vacations<br>• Use English at the airport<br>• Discuss the pros and cons of tourism | Modals of necessity<br>*I* **must** *make a reservation.*<br>Modals of prohibition<br>*You* **must not** *take pictures here.* | Travel preparations<br>Vacations<br>At the airport | Listening for general understanding<br>Conversations: vacations | Planning a dream vacation<br>Making your way through the airport<br>Reduction of *have to, has to, got to* | "Tourists or Trees?"<br>Writing a paragraph about the positive impact of tourism |
| **UNIT 11** | **Careers page 122**<br>• Discuss career choices<br>• Ask and answer job-related questions<br>• Talk about career planning<br>• Identify career qualifications | Modals for giving advice<br>*You* **should** *choose a career that fits your personality.*<br>Indefinite pronouns<br>**Everyone** *in the audience* **was** *laughing.* | Career decisions<br>Participial adjectives | Listening for general understanding<br>An interview: a restaurant owner in Thailand | Role-playing job interviews<br>Intonation in questions | "Maria Fadiman: Ethnobotanist"<br>Filling-out a *dream job* questionnaire |
| **UNIT 12** | **Celebrations page 134**<br>• Describe a festival<br>• Compare holidays in different countries<br>• Talk about personal celebrations<br>• Share holiday traditions | *As … as*<br>*New Year's is* **as** *exciting* **as** *National Day.*<br>*Would rather*<br>*I'd* **rather** *have a big party.* | Festivals and holidays<br>Greetings for celebrations | Listening for general and specific information<br>Discussions: local celebrations or holidays | Comparing different international celebrations<br>Question intonation with lists | "Starting a New Tradition"<br>Writing a substantiated opinion |

**Baltimore, U.S.A.**
How do animals feel about living in a zoo? One man is trying to make their lives better. *Happy Elephants*

**San Salvador, Bahamas**
Do you know the facts about Columbus? Journey back in time as you learn about this explorer. *Columbus and the New World*

**Washington, D.C.**
As everyone knows, only humans use language. But is someone else trying to learn our way of communicating? *Orangutan Language*

**Trinidad and Tobago**
On the island of Trinidad, one man gets up with the sun to watch and wait. Join him as he gets the perfect shot. *Trinidad Bird Man*

**Fes, Morocco**
One of the oldest cities in the world is disappearing, one little piece at a time. What is happening to Fes? *Fes*

# Your World!

**Nubia, Egypt**
In the south of Egypt, a wedding lasts for seven days and seven nights. Join the party! *Nubian Wedding*

**Ulan Bator, Mongolia**
Mongolia is the site of one of the most exciting horse races in the world. Find out what makes it so unusual. *Young Riders of Mongolia*

**Malaysian Borneo**
Something smells strange in Malaysian Borneo. Find out what kind of fruit is causing all the trouble. *Forbidden Fruit*

**Democratic Republic of the Congo**
A scientist tries to cross 2000 miles of African jungle—on foot. What will he find? *Megatransect Project*

**Coober Pedy, Australia**
What could make some people spend their lives underground? Find out what the residents of Coober Pedy, Australia, are looking for. *Coober Pedy Opals*

**Queenstown, New Zealand**
A small town in New Zealand is called the "Adventure Capital of the World." Why do thousands of people go there every year? *Adventure Capital of the World*

= Sites of the video clips you will view in World English 2.

# FOOD FROM

1. What words best describe each picture?

   mountainous   dry   humid   flat
   hot   coastal region   cold   grassland

2. What kind of food do people probably eat in these places?

## UNIT GOALS

Compare what people usually do with
   what they are doing now
Identify regional staple foods
Talk about traditional family dishes
Understand how a regional food becomes
   an international dish

# THE EARTH

## Vocabulary

**A.** Read part of a travel blog.

This is my first visit to Argentina. It's a wonderful place! The people are friendly and the **meals** are delicious—from my morning coffee to my dinner in the evening. The **staple foods** in different parts of the country depend on the **geography** and **climate.** For example, in the northeast, the land is **flat** and the weather is hot and **humid. Farmers** there grow a lot of rice, and people in that **region** eat rice almost every day. Wheat and corn grow well in the cooler central part of the country, so while I'm here I'm eating bread and pasta. In the **coastal** region near the Atlantic Ocean, fish is an everyday food. In the dry **grasslands**, animals such as cattle and sheep are raised. Farmers in **mountainous** regions of Argentina work very hard. They grow **crops,** such as grapes, on small areas of flat land called terraces. All of these different regions and different foods make Argentina a great choice for travelers.

**B.** Write the words in **blue** next to the correct meanings.

1. very important foods _____
2. people who produce food
   _____
3. describes an area near the ocean _____
4. describes an area without mountains _____
5. plants grown for food
   _____
6. the study of the surface of the earth _____

7. breakfast, lunch, and dinner
   _____
8. describes an area with mountains _____
9. a large area _____
10. normal weather patterns
    _____
11. describes air that is moist
    _____
12. grassy areas _____

## Grammar: Simple present tense vs. present continuous tense

| Simple present tense | | Present continuous tense | |
|---|---|---|---|
| I **eat** rice | | I'm **eating** rice | |
| She **cooks** fish | every day. | She's **cooking** fish | now. |
| They **bake** bread | | They**'re baking** bread | |
| We **have** fruit for breakfast | | We**'re having** mangos for breakfast | |

*We use the simple present tense to talk about habits and things that are always true.
*We use the present continuous tense to talk about things that are happening now.

**A.** Complete the paragraph. Use the simple present or present continuous form of the verb in parentheses.

My name _____ (be) Celia Rojas, and I _____ (live) in Mexico City. Here in Mexico, corn _____ (be) a staple food. Many Mexican people _____ (eat) corn tortillas every day. Right now, I _____ (work) in the kitchen with my mother. We _____ (make) enchiladas out of tortillas, chicken, and chili sauce. Our main meal of the day _____ (be) not in the evening. We usually _____ (eat) at around two thirty or three in the afternoon.

▲ Enchiladas with green chili sauce and rice

 **B.** Take turns with a partner doing the following.

1. Tell your partner what you usually eat for breakfast and lunch. (Use the simple present tense.)
2. Tell your partner three things people you know are doing right now. (Use the present continuous tense.)

## Conversation

Track 1-2

**A.** Close your book and listen to the conversation. What do Julie's cousins usually eat?

| | |
|---|---|
| **Tom:** | What are you doing? |
| **Julie:** | I'm looking at pictures from my vacation. |
| **Tom:** | Oh, can I see? Where did you go? |
| **Julie:** | I visited my cousins in the south. It's very flat there. No mountains or hills, and it's pretty dry for most of the year. |
| **Tom:** | What about food? What do your cousins usually eat? |
| **Julie:** | Meals are very simple there. It's basically meat and potatoes and a lot of vegetables. But they grow wheat everywhere, so pasta is becoming popular. |
| **Tom:** | That sounds good. |
| **Julie:** | Yes, I really like the food there. |

 **B.** Practice the conversation with a partner. Switch roles and practice it again.

 **Goal 1** **Compare what people usually do with what people are doing now**

Talk to a partner. What do people usually eat where you live? Then pretend it's a special day or holiday. What are people eating right now?

▲ A worker harvests olives in an olive grove.

## Listening

 **A.** Discuss these questions with a partner.

1. Where do farmers grow rice?
2. Why do they grow it there?

**B.** Listen to the interview of a rice farmer. Circle the correct letter.

Track 1-3

1. Who is the interviewer talking to?
   a. a restaurant owner
   b. a rice farmer
   c. a news reporter
2. What is happening in the rice paddy today?
   a. People are putting rice plants in the ground.
   b. People are planting seeds in the ground.
   c. People are letting water into the rice paddy.
3. What kind of climate does rice need?
   a. hot and dry
   b. warm and wet
   c. cool and humid

**C.** Listen again and answer the questions.

Track 1-3

1. Why doesn't the rice farmer plant seeds like other farmers?

   _____

2. How is the rainfall this year? _____
3. What happens to the water in the rice paddy after the rice plants grow?

   _____

4. What happens to the rice plants after they're dry? _____

### Word Focus

Farmers **raise crops** or **grow crops.**

### Engage!

Do you think farmers and scientists need to find ways to increase food production? Why?

▲ A man works in a rice paddy in Taiwan.

# Communication

 Talk with a partner about two different regions in your country. Describe the land, the climate, and the food.

|  | Region #1 | Region #2 |
|---|---|---|
| land |  |  |
| climate |  |  |
| staple foods |  |  |

# Pronunciation: Linking words together

When a word ends in a consonant sound, and the next word starts with a vowel sound, the words are linked together.

**We cut the rice plants and clean them.**    **We grow a lot of rice.**

Track 1-4

**A.** Listen to the sentences. Notice the pronunciation of the underlined words. Listen again and repeat the sentences.

1. I usually like a tomato with breakfast.
2. Staple foods are the most important foods.
3. We're eating dinner now.
4. Paul and I don't like fish very much.
5. Farmers work on weekends and holidays.
6. Rain falls in all regions of the world.

 **B.** Underline the sounds that link together. Then read the sentences to a partner.

1. Hal enjoys pizza.
2. Wheat bread is very popular.
3. Corn grows well in Mexico.
4. A cheese and tomato sandwich is my favorite lunch.
5. My friend is eating pasta.
6. Dry grasslands are good places to raise animals.

✓ **Goal 2**   **Identify regional staple foods**

Talk to your partner about the staple foods in your region and your country. Give reasons why these foods are staples.

Corn

Wheat

Rice

Oats    Millet

Soybeans

Lentils    Black Beans    Red Beans

Potatoes    Yucca

Yams

## Language Expansion: Staple food crops

**A.** What do you know about staple food crops?
Circle **T** for *true* or **F** for *false*.

| | | | |
|---|---|---|---|
| 1. | Potatoes are originally from South America. | T | F |
| 2. | India is one of the world's largest producers of wheat. | T | F |
| 3. | Lentils are a kind of legume. | T | F |
| 4. | Soy sauce is made from soybeans. | T | F |
| 5. | Yucca grows under the ground. | T | F |
| 6. | China is the world's largest consumer of rice. | T | F |

**B.** Talk to a partner. Which of these staple foods do you eat?

I eat wheat bread almost every day.

Sometimes I eat potatoes.

## Grammar: Simple past tense

| Simple past tense | |
|---|---|
| We **learned** how to make pizza<br>Too much rain **fell**<br>I **ate** sushi for the first time | yesterday.<br>last November.<br>in 2006. |
| *Some verbs are regular in the simple past tense. They have an *-ed* ending. | *Some verbs are irregular in the simple past tense. They have many different forms. |
| learn – learned    travel – traveled<br>arrive – arrived    want – wanted<br>play – played        need – needed<br>ask – asked          help – helped | see – saw        send – sent<br>eat – ate        give – gave<br>drink – drank    take – took<br>go – went        fall – fell |

**A.** Complete the conversation. Use the simple past tense of the verbs in parentheses.

**Mary:** Tell me about yourself, Pedro.

**Pedro:** Well, I love to travel. Last year I _____ (travel) to Lebanon.

**Mary:** Wow! You _____ (go) to Lebanon?

**Pedro:** Yes, and I _____ (meet) my friend Habib and his family there. They _____ (show) me around Beirut and _____ (introduce) me to many new foods.

**Mary:** That sounds like fun.

**Pedro:** It was. I _____ (eat) hummus and falafel, and I _____ (try) a dish made from rice and grape leaves. It _____ (be) delicious!

**B.** Complete these sentences about the past. Use your own information.

1. Yesterday, I ate _____ .
2. Last week, I went _____ .
3. On the first day of this class, I learned _____ .
4. Last month, _____ .
5. In 2008, _____ .

**Real Language**

When we say something is *made from* other things, we're talking about its ingredients.

## Conversation

Track 1-5

**A.** Close your book and listen to the conversation. What is Albert eating? What is it made from?

**Albert:** You should try this! My aunt made it.

**Mary:** Mmmm . . . Delicious! What is it?

**Albert:** It's called *couscous*. It's made from wheat.

**Mary:** And what's this on top of the couscous?

**Albert:** Mostly vegetables and some kind of sauce.

**Mary:** How did your aunt learn to cook it?

**Albert:** Her great-uncle married a woman from North Africa. That's where couscous is from. They always ate it on special occasions.

**Mary:** What an interesting family history!

**Albert:** Yeah, and a great family recipe.

▲ North African couscous

 **B.** Practice the conversation. Switch roles and practice it again.

✓ **Goal 3**  **Talk about traditional family dishes**

Tell your partner about a dish you know how to make. How did you learn to make it?

## Reading

**A.** Look at the timeline and fill in the blanks.

1. Many Italians moved to the United States during _____.
2. People first baked flat bread during _____.
3. People in Naples, Italy, used hot lava to bake pizzas in _____.
4. European explorers went to the Americas during _____.
5. Lombardi's pizza restaurant opened in New York in _____.

 **B.** Fill in the blank with the correct word.

1. Stone Age people baked flat bread on hot _____.
2. _____ were the first people to eat tomatoes.
3. At first, Europeans didn't eat tomatoes because they thought they were _____.
4. In Naples, pizza makers used _____ to heat rocks for their ovens.
5. _____ brought pizza to the United States.

**C.** Talk to a partner. Make a list of foods that are popular in your country that people brought from other countries. Where did these foods come from?

> People here eat a lot of curry. I think curry came from India.

> Right. There's an Indian restaurant downtown. They have wonderful curry.

## Communication

Work in a small group. Invent a new kind of pizza for Lombardi's restaurant. You should all agree on the toppings, the sauce, and the type of crust.

☐ Naples, Italy

# A Slice of History

What do you like on your pizza? Cheese? Tomatoes? Pineapple? People may disagree on their favorite ingredients, but many people agree that pizza is a favorite food. Where and when did people start making pizza? To find out, we have to travel back in time. People were baking bread dough on hot rocks in the Stone Age.

Stone Age people gathered ancient types of wheat and other grains. They mixed the grains into a batter. Then they poured the batter onto rocks in their campfires. What they got was a flat bread—the first pizza crust. In time, prehistoric bakers started using the flat bread as a plate. They put other food, herbs, and spices on the bread. Then they ate it.

Over the centuries, tastes changed. In the 1500s, European explorers tried to find a better way to sail to Asia to buy spices. Instead, they found a way to the Americas. Native American people in Peru, Central America, and Mexico enjoyed eating tomatoes, but in Europe, people thought tomatoes were poisonous! With time, Europeans and other people discovered

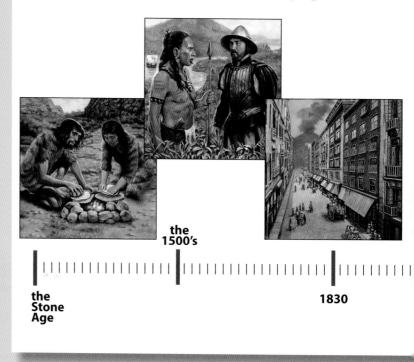

the 1500's

the Stone Age    1830

that tomatoes were delicious and safe to eat. Cooks in Naples, an Italian city, began putting tomatoes onto baking dough.

People in Naples didn't stop there, however. They took another big step in pizza history. The world's first true pizza shop opened in Naples in 1830. Cooking pizza in Naples wasn't as easy as it is today. It was even a little dangerous. You see, pizza makers didn't use wood, gas, or electric ovens. Instead they used lava from a nearby volcano to heat rocks for baking pizza dough. Despite the danger, pizza was soon a big hit. People ate it for lunch and dinner. They even ate it for breakfast. News of the pizza shop spread quickly, and people traveled to Naples to try the tasty dish.

In the late 1800s, many Italians moved to the United States. They brought pizza with them. The first American pizzeria was Lombardi's in New York City. It opened its doors in 1905. Now pizza is one of the top three most popular U.S. foods. Of course, Americans are hardly the only pizza lovers. Humans eat 5 billion pizzas a year. Our choices for toppings vary widely. Brazilians love green peas on their pizza. Russians like fish and onions. People in India use lamb and tofu. Some pizzas truly sound strange. Yet all share two things. Each begins with bread. And each is a slice of history.

1905

the late 1800s — the present

## Writing

Read the email and write a response. Be sure to answer all the questions.

**From:** Ronald Ferguson

**To:** _____

**Subject:** Help! My students have some questions for you.

Hi there,

How is everything there? I hope you're doing well, and I hope you can answer some questions from my students. As you know, our class will visit your country next month, and the students are asking me about the food. Here are some of their questions:

What do people usually eat for breakfast there?
Do you have pizza and burger restaurants?
What are some traditional dishes we can try?
Is there a staple food that people eat every day?
What are some good things to eat for lunch and dinner?

Thank you very much! I look forward to our visit next month. Maybe you can join us for a good meal.
Your friend,
Ronald

**From:** _____
**To:** Ronald Ferguson
**Subject: RE:** Help! My students have some questions for you.

_____

_____

_____

✓ **Goal 4** | **Understand how a regional food becomes an international dish**

Talk with a partner. Is there a food from your region or country that is popular in other countries? Why do you think this food is popular in other countries?

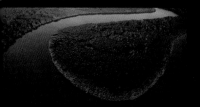

## Before You Watch

**A.** Write each of the following adjectives in the appropriate column.

| smelly | delicious | fragrant | disgusting |

| Positive meaning | Negative meaning |
| --- | --- |
| | |

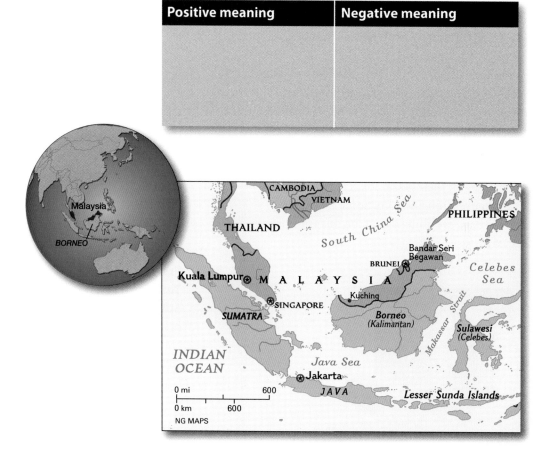

 **B.** Discuss the following questions with a partner.

1. What are some foods that have a very strong smell?
2. After you prepare food with a strong smell in your home, how can you get rid of the odor?

## While You Watch

**A.** Watch the video, *Forbidden Fruit*. Match the people to the actions.

1. Hotel staff ____
2. Hotel guests ____
3. Hotel cleaning staff ____

a. try to bring durian fruit into hotel rooms.
b. use a special machine in smelly hotel rooms.
c. watch for people bringing in durian fruit.

**B.** Read the summary of the video and fill in the blanks with words from the box. Then watch the video again and check your answers.

| vigil | smuggle | front lines | alert | invasion | war |

▲ a floating market

## Video Summary

The video looks at the problem of hotel guests in Malaysian Borneo bringing smelly durian fruit into their rooms. It presents the problem in terms of warfare. For example, durian season is a seasonal _____. Guests _____ the fruit into their rooms like spies with secret information for a general. The hotels are on the _____ of the durian _____, which means they are the ones doing most of the fighting. The hotel managers maintain a constant _____, watching and waiting for anyone with durian fruit in their bags. And when a guest does get durian fruit past the hotel staff, there is a durian _____, or an emergency situation.

## After You Watch

Write a guide for tourists visiting your country.
1. Describe three foods that are popular in your culture, but that people from other cultures might find disgusting or intolerable.
2. Give reasons why tourists should try those foods.

## Communication

You are a group of hotel owners in Malaysian Borneo. Brainstorm a list of ways to prevent people from bringing durian fruit into their hotel rooms.

# COMMUNICATION

1. Which of these things are the same in all countries? Which of them are sometimes different?
   a. gestures
   b. smile
   c. eye contact
   d. greetings

2. Have you met someone from another country? What did you talk about?

## UNIT GOALS

Communicate with people from different cultures

Make small talk with new people

Use small talk to *break the ice*

Learn how professionals *break the ice*

# UNIT 2

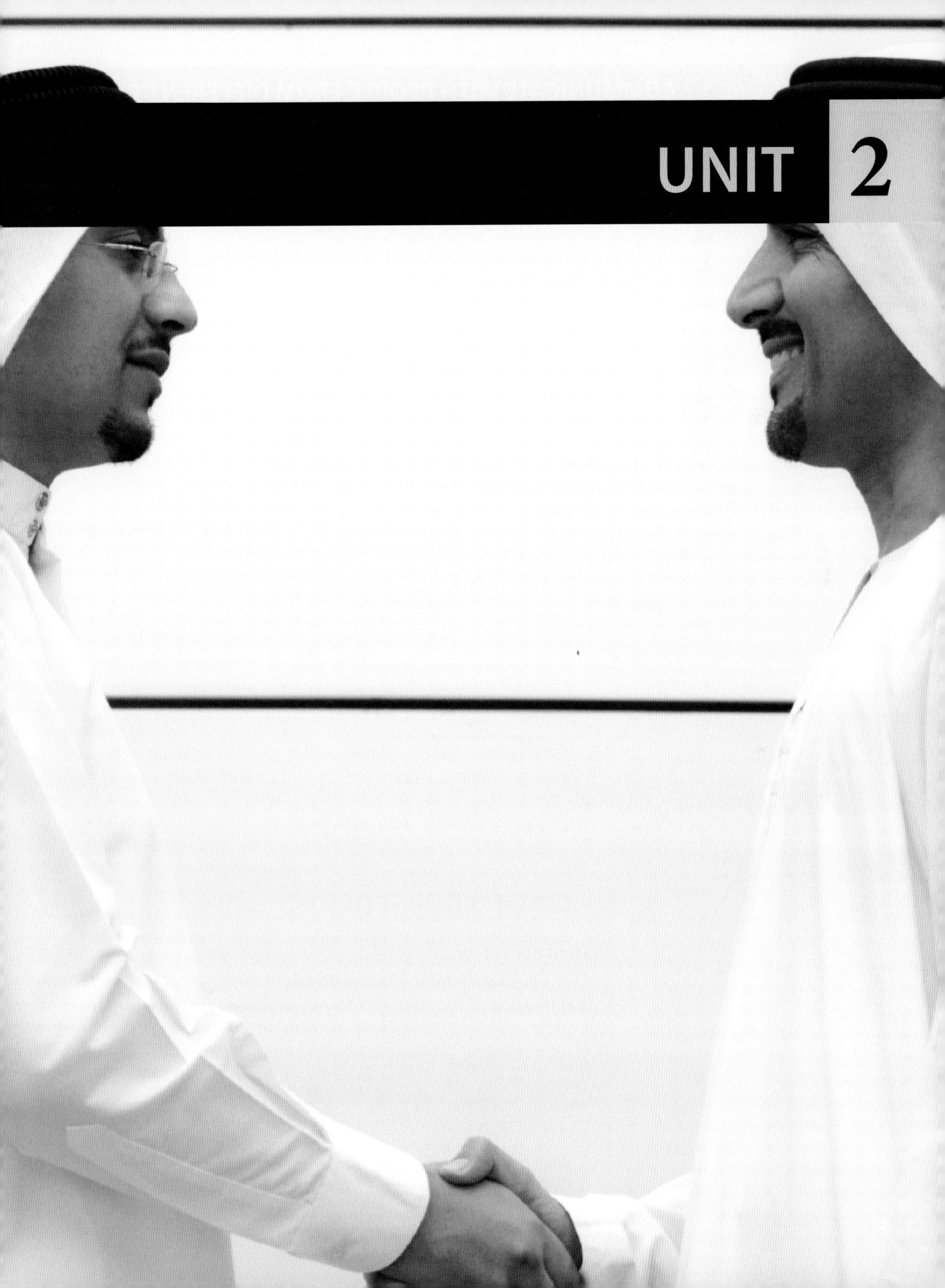

## Vocabulary

**A.** Read the article.

Every **culture** around the world has different **customs** and ways of communicating.

When you learn to communicate in a language, you learn a lot of **rules**. You learn what kind of greetings to use in different situations. For example, in English, we say "Hi!" in an **informal** situation. In a more **formal** situation, we shake hands and say "How do you do?" In China, a **traditional** greeting is "Have you eaten today?" After that, there are rules for making **small talk** when you meet a new person.

People in different cultures also have different ways of using their bodies to communicate. But there's one kind of communication that's the same everywhere. A smile can always **connect** people.

**B.** Write the words in **blue** next to the correct meanings.

1. the correct way to do something
   _____

2. bring together  _____

3. very serious and important
   _____

4. people with the same language and way of living _____

5. activities that are usual in a country _____

6. the same for a long time without changing _____

7. conversation about things that aren't important _____

8. friendly and relaxed  _____
   _____

### Word Focus

**follow** + **a rule** = do something the correct way

**make** + **small talk** = talk about things that aren't important

## Grammar: Present perfect tense

**Present perfect tense**

Subject + **has/have** + (**not**) + past participle

He **has traveled** to many countries. He **has not been** in Korea before.

We use the present perfect tense:
*to talk about something that started in the past and continues now.
*to talk about something that happened several times in the past.
*to talk about something in the past that is connected with the present.

**A.** Complete the sentences. Use the present perfect form of the verb in parentheses.

1. I _____ (meet) many Bahrainis, but I _____ (be, not) in Bahrain.
2. My husband and I _____ (be) married for six years.
3. Mari isn't in the office this week. She _____ (go) on vacation.
4. Ahmad doesn't want to watch TV. He _____ (watch) TV every night this week.
5. Tomorrow is my friend's graduation, but I _____ (buy, not) her a present. I forgot!
6. I _____ (finish) all my homework. Now I can go out.

**B.** Finish writing the following questions. Then ask a partner to answer them. Write some questions of your own.

Have you ever eaten Indian food?

No, never.

Yes, once/many times. It's really good!

Have you ever . . .

1. eaten _____ food?
2. seen a movie from _____ (country)?
3. gone to _____ ?
4. played _____ ?
5. talked to _____ ?

## Conversation

Track 1-6

**A.** Close your book and listen to the conversation. Why is the woman worried?

**Annie:** Guess what? I'm going to spend a month in Mexico City.

**Rick:** That's great! What are you going to do there?

**Annie:** I'm going to work in my company's office there. I'm a little worried, though. I've never been to Mexico before.

**Rick:** But you've met lots of people from Mexico, and you've taken Spanish lessons.

**Annie:** That's true. And I guess I've learned something about Mexican customs.

**Rick:** It sounds to me like you're ready to go.

**B.** Practice the conversation with a partner.

▲ aerial view of Mexico City

## ✓ Goal 1  **Communicate with people from different cultures**

Take turns pretending to be a foreigner coming to your country for a month. Talk to your partner about some customs that might surprise you and some things that you have done to prepare for the trip.

## Listening

Track 1-7

**A.** These people are meeting for the first time. Listen to their conversations. Where are the people?

**Conversation 1** The speakers are in ___.
    a. a hospital    b. a school    c. an airport

**Conversation 2** These people are in ___.
    a. a restaurant    b. an apartment    c. an office building

Track 1-7

**B.** Listen again. What do the people make small talk about?

**Conversation 1** They make small talk about ___.
    a. classes    b. weather    c. clothes

**Conversation 2** They make small talk about ___.
    a. sports    b. TV shows    c. the neighborhood

**C.** What will they talk about next? Think of two more ideas for each conversation.

## Pronunciation: *Have* or *has* vs. contractions

In statements with the present perfect verb tense, **have** and **has** are sometimes pronounced, but when people speak quickly, contractions are used.

Track 1-8

**A.** Listen and repeat.

| *Have* or *has* | Contraction |
| --- | --- |
| I have | I've |
| you have | you've |
| we have | we've |
| they have | they've |
| she has | she's |
| he has | he's |
| it has | it's |

Track 1-9

**B.** Listen and circle the sentence you hear.

1. a. I have never gone skiing.    b. I've never gone skiing.
2. a. He has been to Colombia three times.    b. He's been to Colombia three times.
3. a. Linda has taken a scuba diving class.    b. Linda's taken a scuba diving class.
4. a. They have already eaten breakfast.    b. They've already eaten breakfast.
5. a. We have had three tests this week.    b. We've had three tests this week.
6. a. Michael has found a new job.    b. Michael's found a new job.

# Communication

**A.** Read the information.

English-speakers often make small talk when they meet someone new. They ask questions to get to know the other person. At school, people often talk about their classes. At work, people talk about their jobs. They don't talk about very personal subjects. For example, "Which department do you work in?" is a good question, but "How much money do you make?" is too personal.

 **B.** Circle the topics that are good for small talk when you meet someone for the first time. Then add two more ideas.

school    money    family    work    sports    religion

_____    _____

 **C.** Read the situations. Choose a question to ask for each situation. Then practice conversations with a partner.

**Situation 1** At work, Mouna talks to Judy. It's Judy's first day at her job.
    a. How old are you?          b. Are you new in this city?

**Situation 2** Saleh is from Oman. He talks to Abdul at the International Students' Club. It's Abdul's first meeting.
    a. Where are you from?          b. Do you like sports?

**Situation 3** Mark lives in apartment 104. He meets Abbas, his new neighbor, in the apartment building.
    a. Which apartment do you live in?          b. Are you a student?

 **D.** Which are good questions to ask when you meet someone new? Circle the letters.

    a.  Which classes are you taking now?
    b.  Who is your teacher?
    c.  What was your score on the placement test?
    d.  Have you studied at this school before?
    e.  When did you start working here?
    f.  How much did you pay for that car?
    g.  Have you lived here for a long time?
    h.  How much money do you earn here?

 **Goal 2    Make small talk with new people**

Pretend you are meeting your classroom partner for the first time (on the first day of class, waiting for the bus, or in another situation). Talk for two minutes.

# Language Expansion: Starting a conversation

**A.** Read the questions in the box. Think of different ways to answer them.

> **Starting a conversation**
> How do you like this weather?
> Where do you know Mary from? (the office)
> Are you enjoying yourself? (at a festival)
> Has it been a long week? (at work or school)
> Did you hear about _____? (something that happened in the news)
> How long have you been waiting? (for the elevator, the bus, the meeting to begin, etc.)

 **B.** Choose one of the situations. Start a conversation with a partner. Try to make small talk for as long as you can. Then change partners and practice again with another situation.

| waiting in line in the office cafeteria | walking in the park |
|---|---|
| at a welcoming event for new students | at the airport |

# Grammar: Signal words: *Already, ever, yet*

| *Already/ever/yet* + the present perfect tense | | |
|---|---|---|
| *already* | **Has** Ahmad **already left**? | question |
| | We **have already studied** this. | affirmative statement |

*We use *already* to talk about something that happened in the past. It is used for emphasis in questions and affirmative statements.

| *ever/never* | **Have** you **ever** seen a giraffe? | questions |
|---|---|---|
| *never/not ever* | We **have never** played tennis in the rain. | negative statements |
| | We **haven't ever** gone to Canada. | |
| *yet/not yet* | **Have** you **done** the dishes **yet**? | questions |
| | Alima **hasn't eaten** lunch **yet**. | negative statements |

*We use *ever/never* (*not ever*) in questions or negative statements to talk about something that has or hasn't happened at any time before now.
*We use *yet/not yet* in questions or negative statements for emphasis.

**A.** Read the page from Marcy's journal. What things has she already done in her life? Complete the sentences.

1. She has already _____ .
2. She has already _____ .
3. She has already _____ .
4. She has already _____ .

_Things I Want to Do in My Life_

learn to speak English ✓
learn to speak Arabic
visit my cousins in Tunisia
eat traditional food from Japan ✓
learn to be more polite when I say "no" to people
go swimming in the ocean ✓
learn how to drive a car ✓
buy a car
take a scuba diving class

**B.** Read the conversation Marcy has with a classmate. Fill in the blanks.

**John:** Have you ever traveled to another country?
**Marcy:** No, I have _____ left this country, but I want to go to Tunisia some day.
**John:** Have _____ ever learned to speak a new language?
**Marcy:** I think I have _____ to speak English pretty well.
**John:** _____ you ever eaten any unusual food?
**Marcy:** Yes! I have _____ Japanese _miso_ soup and _udon_ noodles.
**John:** What about driving? Can you drive a car?
**Marcy:** Well, I learned how to drive a car last year, but I _____ bought one yet.

**C.** Take turns. Ask a partner questions about the people below with _have/has_ and _ever_. Answer using _no, never_, and contractions.

| Mrs. Cooper | I | Mr. Muramoto |
|---|---|---|
| Tom and Rita | you and I | your friends |
| you | our English teacher | Ms. Sanchez |

**Has** Mrs. Cooper **ever** taken a cooking class?

**No, she's never** taken a cooking class.

## Conversation

**A.** Close your book and listen to the conversation. What do the speakers decide to do about the homework?

Track 1-10

**Tom:** Excuse me. Are you in my history class?
**Rita:** Yes! I saw you in class yesterday. I'm Rita.
**Tom:** Hi, Rita. I'm Tom. Is this your first class with Mr. Olsen?
**Rita:** Yes, it is, but I've heard good things about him. What about you?
**Tom:** I've taken his classes before, and they've always been good.
**Rita:** That's nice. Have you already done the homework for tomorrow?
**Tom:** No, not yet. What about you?
**Rita:** Not yet. Maybe we can call each other if we have any problems with it.
**Tom:** That's a great idea! I'll give you my number.

**B.** Practice the conversation. Then practice the conversation with subjects you are studying and teachers from your school.

**Have** you **ever** taken a class with Ms. Lee before?

Yes, I took an art class with her.

✓ **Goal 3**   **Use small talk to _break the ice_**

Move around the class. Walk up to five classmates and ask them an _icebreaker_ question.

## Reading

**A.** Discuss these questions with a partner.

1. Have you ever taken a picture of people you didn't know? How did you do it?
2. What kinds of photographs do you like? What makes those photographs good?

**B.** Circle **T** for *true* or **F** for *false*. Then correct the false sentences.

1. Belt has never traveled to England.    T   F
2. Belt has never traveled to Antarctica.    T   F
3. Petra is a very old city in Jordan.    T   F
4. Belt can only connect with English-speakers.    T   F
5. People can connect with each other in bad weather.    T   F
6. Volunteering is one way to begin a photography career.    T   F

**C.** Tell a partner about some places you have traveled. Then talk about some places you haven't visited yet, but that you want to visit.

Around the World

# Taking Pictures of the World

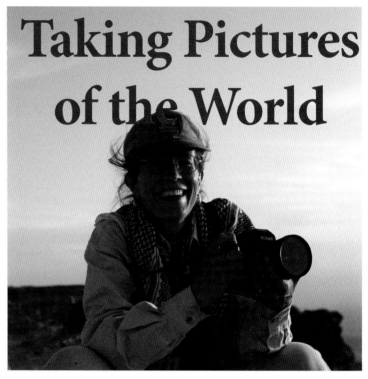

▲ Annie Griffiths Belt

Meet Annie Griffiths Belt, a National Geographic photographer. Belt has worked for National Geographic since 1978, and has taken pictures on almost every continent in the world. In fact, Antarctica is the only continent Belt hasn't seen yet.

Belt's photographs are well known for their beauty and high quality. They also reflect very different cultures and regions of the world. Belt has photographed the ancient city of Petra, Jordan, as well as the green landscapes of the Lake District in England. Recently, her pictures appeared in a book about undeveloped natural places in North America.

Everywhere that Belt goes, she takes pictures of people. Belt has found ways to connect with people of all ages and nationalities even when she does not speak their language. "The greatest privilege of my job is being allowed into people's lives," she has said. "The camera is like a passport, and I am often overwhelmed by how quickly people welcome me."

Knowing how to *break the ice* has helped to make Belt a successful photographer, but experts say that anyone can learn to connect with new people. When people speak the same language, greetings and small talk can make strangers feel more comfortable with each other. When people don't speak the same language, a smile is very helpful. Having something in common can also help *break the ice*. For example, Belt has traveled with her two children, so when she takes pictures of children or their parents, they all have that family connection in common. Even bad weather can help people to connect when they are experiencing it together.

Belt has some advice if you are thinking about a career in photography. You can volunteer to take pictures for a local organization that can't afford to hire a professional photographer. You can also take a good, honest look at your best photographs. If you're a real photographer, your photos are good because of your personal and technical skills. Belt also recommends studying and learning from photos taken by professional photographers.

Remember, the next time you look at a beautiful photograph, you might be looking at the work of Annie Griffiths Belt. And the next time you meet a new person, don't be afraid to *break the ice*. The connection you make could be very rewarding.

▲ Portrait by Annie Griffiths Belt

▲ The ancient city of Petra in Jordan taken by Annie Griffiths Belt

# Writing

**A.** Complete the sentences with your own ideas.

1. Annie Griffiths Belt's work is interesting because _____.
2. For me, traveling is _____ because _____.
3. For me, connecting with new people is _____ because _____.
4. Belt takes good "people pictures" because _____.
5. My own photographs are usually ____ _____ _____.
6. The next time I need to *break the ice*, I will _____ _____.

 **B.** Share your sentences with a partner. Talk about your ideas.

✓ **Goal 4** | **Learn how professionals *break the ice***

In what professions do people need to ***break the ice*** quickly in order to do their jobs? Talk with your partner about different ways they can do this.

# Before You Watch

Read about the video and check the meanings of the words in bold.

Orangutans are large, intelligent **primates**. At the National Zoo in Washington, D.C., Rob Shumaker runs the Orangutan Language Project. Of course, orangutans aren't able to speak like humans. They can, however, learn to connect **symbols** to objects. In human language, words are also symbols for the real objects they represent. Shumaker believes the language program is mentally **stimulating** for the orangutans. The program is completely **voluntary**, so the animals can choose to participate or not, and it's part of a zoo **exhibit** called Think Tank, which helps to educate people about the problems orangutans face in the wild.

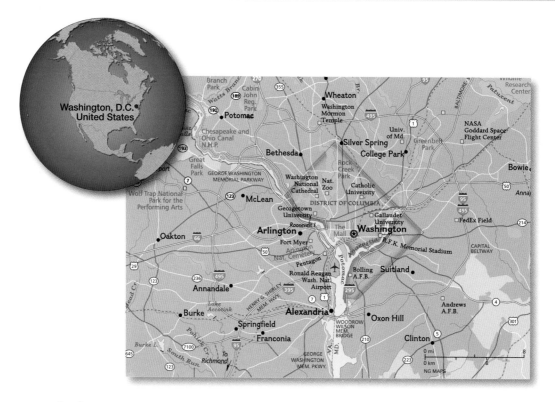

# While You Watch

**A.** Watch the video *Orangutan Language*. Circle each word when you first hear it.

| exhibit | symbols | voluntary | primates | stimulating |
| --- | --- | --- | --- | --- |

 **B.** Watch the video again and circle the correct answers.

1. In Malay, the word *orangutan* means "person of the (jungle/forest)."
2. The orangutans in the video are Inda and (Miki/Azie).
3. The orangutans work with symbols on (a computer/paper).
4. The orangutans are (brother and sister/mother and son).
5. Wild orangutans could become extinct in (10 to 12/8 to 10) years

**C.** Watch the video again and answer the questions.

1. Where do orangutans come from? _____
   _____
2. What choices does the zoo give the orangutans? _____
   _____
3. How old is Inda, the female orangutan? _____
4. Can the orangutans use symbols to make sentences? _____
   _____
5. What do zoo officials hope exhibits like Think Tank will do? _____
   _____

▲ Shumaker and Inda perform certain exercises on the computer.

## After You Watch

 Brainstorm several ways that animals communicate. Do you think animal communication is very different from human communication?

## Communication

 Any writing system is a set of symbols. You have the opportunity to create a new way to write English.

1. Think of 10 English words that are difficult to spell.
2. Make a word list with a better way to write the words.
3. Share your word list with the class. (Can your classmates guess all the words?)

# CITIES

1. What word best describes each picture?
   a. skyscraper
   b. neighborhood
   c. market
   d. downtown

2. What is your city famous for?

## UNIT GOALS

Describe your city or town
Explain what makes a good neighborhood
Discuss an action plan
Make predictions about cities in the future

## Vocabulary

**A.** Read the opinions. Which one do you agree with? Give more reasons.

"**Urban**[a] life is great! There is good **public transportation**[b], like trains and buses. And we also have **freeways**[c] where cars can go fast. People can find good jobs in a **factory**[d] or a shopping center. There is great **cultural life**[e] in theaters and museums. Cities get bigger every year because they are the best place to live."

"City life is terrible! Cities are so **crowded**[f], with too many people in a small area, and the **population**[g] grows every year. There is too much **traffic**[h], because people want to drive their cars everywhere. It's always **noisy**[i] and never quiet. A lot of people want to live in a **rural**[j] area, but there aren't many jobs in the country. It's better to live in a **suburb**[k] outside of the city, and **commute**[l] to a job downtown by car."

**B.** Match the words in blue in exercise **A** to the correct meaning.

1. in the city _a_
2. a town outside of a city ___
3. roads where cars go fast ___
4. travel to your job ___
5. trains, buses, and subways ___
6. a place where workers make things ___
7. the number of people who live in a place ___
8. interesting things to do ___
9. cars moving on a street ___
10. too full ___
11. too loud ___
12. in the country ___

## Grammar: Future with *will*

 **A.** What do you think? Circle **Y** for *yes* or **N** for *no*. Compare your answers with a partner's answers.

In the year 2030 . . .

| | | |
|---|---|---|
| 1. My city will be bigger than it is now. | Y | N |
| 2. People will drive cars in the city. | Y | N |
| 3. Houses will be smaller than they are now. | Y | N |
| 4. The city will have many parks and green spaces. | Y | N |

| *Will* | |
|---|---|
| Statement | The city **will be** cleaner. |
| Negative | People **won't drive** cars. |
| *Yes/no* questions | **Will** houses **be** smaller? |
| *Wh-* questions | Where **will** people live? |

*Use *will* to make predictions about things you are sure about in the future.
*In speaking, use contractions with *will*: *I'll, you'll, he'll, she'll, we'll, they'll.*

**Word Focus**

**traffic** + **jam** = so many cars in the street that they can't move

**population** + **growth** = more people living in a place

**B.** Complete the sentences with *will* and a verb from the box.

| rain | have | not go | take | be | live | not read |
| --- | --- | --- | --- | --- | --- | --- |

1. The TV weather report says it _____ tonight.
2. In 2030, only a few people _____ in rural areas.
3. People _____ newspapers in the future.
4. I think we _____ a test next week.
5. In the future, students _____ to school.
   They _____ classes online.
6. Leila _____ nineteen on her next birthday.

 **C.** Ask a partner three questions about city life in the future. Use *will* in each question.

# Conversation

Track 1-11

**A.** Close your book and listen to the conversation. Where did Mimi live when she was a child?

**Mark:** So, where are you from, Mimi?
**Mimi:** I live in New York now, but I grew up in Seoul.
**Mark:** Really? I've never been to Seoul. What's it like?
**Mimi:** Well, some people think it's too crowded, but it has great restaurants.
**Mark:** I've heard that it's very polluted.
**Mimi:** That's true, but it's changing now. In the future, it will be much cleaner.

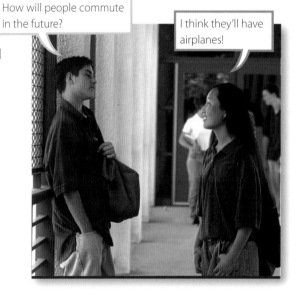

How will people commute in the future?

I think they'll have airplanes!

 **B.** Practice the conversation with a partner. Switch roles and practice it again.

**C.** Check the things that are true about your city. Add two more ideas of your own.

| Bad things about a city | | Good things about a city | |
| --- | --- | --- | --- |
| It's ____. | | It has great ____. | |
| ☐ noisy | ☐ boring | ☐ restaurants | ☐ beaches |
| ☐ dangerous | ☐ crowded | ☐ parks | ☐ museums |
| ☐ expensive | ☐ polluted | ☐ neighborhoods | ☐ culture |
| _____ | _____ | _____ | _____ |

**Real Language**

To ask about a person's hometown or home country, we say *Where are you from?*

## ✓ Goal 1    Describe your city or town

Make a new conversation about your city. Then make new conversations about two other cities you know.

## Listening

▲ Jardin Nomade in Paris

 **A.** Discuss these questions with a partner.

1. How often do you go to a park?
2. What do you do there?
3. What do you think about the parks in your city or town?

**Track 1-12**

**B.** Listen to a radio program about a park in Paris called the Jardin Nomade. Circle the correct letter.

1. The Jardin Nomade is in ___ area.
   a. a rural      b. an urban      c. a suburban
2. The Jardin Nomade is amazing because it's so ___.
   a. big          b. small          c. old
3. In the Jardin Nomade, people ___.
   a. grow food     b. go swimming    c. enjoy art

**Track 1-12**

**C.** Listen again. Answer each question.

1. What year did the park start? _____
2. How many gardens do people have in the park? _____
3. What do the neighbors eat there every month? _____
4. How many people come to the dinners? _____
5. How many parks like this are there in Paris now? _____

## Pronunciation: Emphatic stress

**Engage!**

What are some new things in your city?

**Track 1-13**

**A.** Listen and repeat the exchanges. Notice how the underlined words sound stronger.

1. A: Is your city <u>expensive</u>?
   B: Yes, it's <u>really</u> expensive!

2. A: Do you like living in an <u>apartment</u>?
   B: No, I like living in a <u>house</u> much more.

3. A: Is your neighborhood <u>new</u> or <u>old</u>?
   B: The houses are very <u>old</u>.

4. A: Can you <u>walk</u> to school?
   B: No, I <u>can't</u>. It's too <u>far</u>.

 **B.** Read the exchanges in exercise **A** with a partner. Stress the underlined words.

 **C.** Take turns asking and answering three questions about your neighborhood. Stress the important words.

Are there any <u>parks</u> in your neighborhood?

Yes, there are <u>two</u>.

# Conversation

**A.** Close your book and listen to the conversation. What is the problem in Sarah's neighborhood?

**Ben:** How do you like living in your neighborhood?

**Sarah:** Well, it has a lot of beautiful old buildings, but there are some problems.

**Ben:** Like what?

**Sarah:** It doesn't have many different stores. There's only one supermarket, so food is very expensive.

**Ben:** That sounds like a pretty big problem.

**Sarah:** It is, but the city is building a new shopping center now. Next year, we'll have more stores.

 **B.** Practice the conversation with a partner. Switch roles and practice again.

**C.** Write these words or phrases in the correct column. Add two more ideas to each column.

| beautiful buildings | crime | a lot of noise | heavy traffic |
| public transportation | pollution | trees and green space | many different stores |

| Good things in a neighborhood | Bad things in a neighborhood |
| --- | --- |
|  |  |

 **D.** Make two new conversations. Use your ideas from exercise **C**.

 **E.** Join another pair of students. What are the four most important things for a good neighborhood? Talk about your ideas in exercise **C** and make a new list together. Give reasons.

| Most important things for a good neighborhood | Reason |
| --- | --- |
| 1. |  |
| 2. |  |
| 3. |  |
| 4. |  |

 **Goal 2** **Explain what makes a good neighborhood**

Explain your group's list to the class.

# Language Expansion: Using maps

**A.** Study the map. Write the word from the box in the correct space on the map.

| south |
| symbols |
| east |
| key |
| west |
| scale |

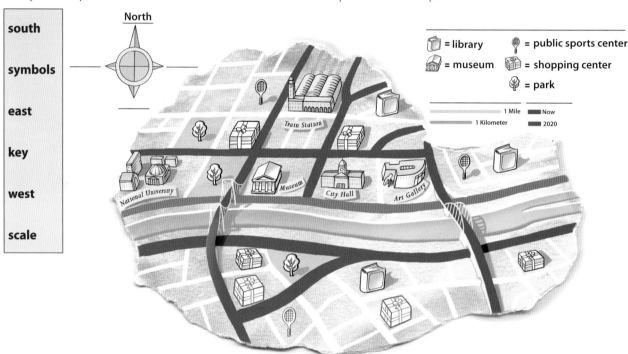

 **B.** Take turns asking and answering the questions.

1. In which parts of the city are the libraries?
2. Where are the public sports centers?
3. Where will the new road be?
4. How many shopping centers does the city have now? How many will it have in 2020?
5. What do you think this city needs?

> Where's the train station?

> It's in the north of the city.

# Grammar: *Will* + time clauses

**A.** Study the sentences and circle the correct letter.

**I will finish my homework <u>before I go to bed</u>.**

1. What will you do first?
   a. Finish my homework.   b. Go to bed.
2. The word *before* is with the action that happens _____.
   a. first   b. second

**I will wash the dishes <u>after I eat dinner</u>.**

1. What will you do first?
   a. Wash the dishes.   b. Eat dinner.
2. The word *after* is with the action that happens _____.
   a. first   b. second

## Time clauses

I'll look at the neighborhood carefully **before I choose a new apartment**.
**Before I choose a new apartment**, I'll look at the neighborhood carefully.
I'll meet my neighbors **after I move into my new apartment**.
**After I move into my new apartment**, I'll meet my neighbors.

* A time clause tells when something happens. Use *before* and *after* at the beginning of a time clause.
* In a sentence with *will*, use the present tense in the time clause.
* The time clause can come first or second in the sentence. If the time clause is first, it is followed by a comma.

 **B.** Use the information in the note with time clauses to tell your partner your plans.

1. find a place for the meeting/make an invitation (after)
2. make a list of things to talk about/give invitations to all the neighbors (before)
3. make a list of things to talk about/have the meeting (before)
4. have the meeting/ask the city government for a sports center (after)
5. talk to newspaper reporters/ask the city government for a sports center (after)

*We need a sports center in our neighborhood!*

May 2 find a place for the meeting
May 3 make an invitation
May 5–12 give invitations to all the neighbors
May 13 make a list of things to talk about
May 25 have the meeting
May 26 ask the city government for a sports center
May 27 talk to newspaper reporters

## Conversation

 **A.** Practice the conversation. What does Jennie want for her neighborhood?

**Jennie:** This neighborhood really needs a library.
**Dan:** You're absolutely right. But how can we get one?
**Jennie:** I think we should have a neighborhood meeting to talk about it.
**Dan:** That's a good idea. And after we have the meeting, we'll write a letter to the newspaper.
**Jennie:** Great! I'll help you.

 **B.** Make new conversations to talk about these neighborhood places.

▲ bicycle paths

 **Goal 3** **Discuss an action plan**

What does your city or neighborhood need? How can you get it?

▲ a playground

slum

garbage dump

running water

hut

resident

São Paulo, Brazil

# Megacities!

São Paulo, Brazil

## Reading

**A.** Guess the answers. Then read the article to check your guesses.

1. The first cities started ___ years ago.
   a. 1000    b. 5000    c. 10,000
2. Every week, ___ people in the world move from rural areas to cities.
   a. 400,000  b. 800,000  c. 1 million
3. The world's largest city is ___.
   a. Tokyo  b. Mexico City  c. New York

**B.** Find the information in the article. All of the answers are numbers.

1. The percentage of people living in cities in 2030 _____
2. The number of megacities in 1995 _____
3. The number of megacities in 2015 _____
4. The population of São Paulo _____
5. The number of people traveling by car in São Paulo _____
6. When Ilson da Silva came to São Paulo _____
7. The number of rooms his house had then _____
8. The number of rooms his house has now _____

Some people love cities, and other people hate them. But more people than ever are choosing to live in one. The first cities started about 5000 years ago. Since then, cities have always been the centers of everything important. The government, businesses, and the university were always in the city. Around the world more than 1 million people every week move from rural areas to cities. In the year 2030, 60 percent of the world's people will live in cities.

These cities will be bigger than ever. A megacity is a city with a population of over 10 million people. In 1995, the world had 14 megacities. In 2015, there will be 21 megacities. And the ranking will continue to change. Today, the world's five largest cities are 1. Tokyo, 2. Mexico City, 3. São Paulo, 4. New York, and 5. Mumbai (Bombay). In 2015, they will probably be 1. Tokyo, 2. Dhaka, 3. Mumbai, 4. São Paulo, and 5. Delhi.

Megacities around the world face the same problems: traffic and housing. São Paulo, Brazil, is a good example. "There are 30 million daily trips in São Paulo," says Jorge Wilheim, a city official. "One-third is public transport, one-third is private cars, and one-third is walking. Sixty to seventy percent should be on public transportation." The city is building a new freeway and adding to the subway system, but it's slow work. Every day, millions of people are sitting in traffic jams.

Housing is also a serious problem for the 18 million people in São Paulo. Most of the jobs are downtown, and houses and apartments are very expensive there. So workers live in cheaper places far away from their jobs and commute for many hours. And many new **residents** can't find any housing for their families, so they live in **slums**. These are places where people find empty land and build small **huts**.

Ilson da Silva is one man who has done this. When he came to the city six years ago, he didn't have a job. He built a one-room hut next to a **garbage dump**. Now he works as a janitor, and his house has three rooms and a flower garden. The government has brought in **running water** and electricity, and the slum is becoming a real neighborhood. For Ilson, and for millions of other people, megacities mean hope for a better future.

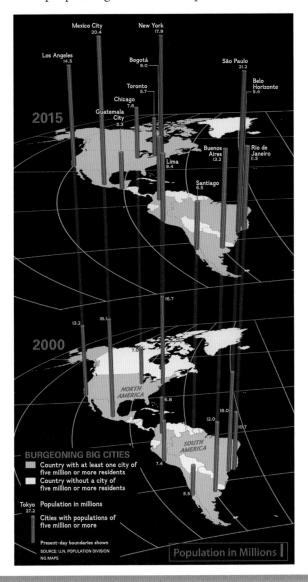

**C.** Discuss these questions with your partner.

1. Why do people move from rural areas to cities?
2. What is better about city life? What is better about rural life?

## Communication

How will your city be different in 2030? Work with a partner and complete the chart with your ideas.

|  | Now | 2030 |
|---|---|---|
| population |  |  |
| housing |  |  |
| transportation |  |  |
| the environment |  |  |
| other things |  |  |

## Writing

What will your city be like in 2030? Write a paragraph using your ideas from the chart.

✓ **Goal 4** **Make predictions about cities in the future**

Read your paragraph to the class.

## Before You Watch

Read about the video and check the meanings of the words in **bold**.

The Bouananiya Medersa in Fes, Morocco, is a **masterpiece** of art. It's in very bad condition now, but people are working to **restore** its walls and **fountains**. Some old buildings in Fes are in danger because **wealthy** people buy and take away pieces of them. Now, **private** organizations are trying to **preserve** these buildings for the future. They hope all people can enjoy Morocco's **heritage**.

## While You Watch

 **A.** Watch the video, *Restoring Fes*. Circle the correct answer.

1. The medina is the (oldest/newest) part of Fes.
2. (Rich/Poor) people live in the medina.

 **B.** Watch the video again. Circle **T** for *true* or **F** for *false*.

| | | |
|---|---|---|
| 1. In the past, the Bouananiya Medersa was a palace. | T | F |
| 2. Restorers are taking old paint off the walls of the Medersa. | T | F |
| 3. The government isn't interested in restoring historic buildings in Fes. | T | F |
| 4. There is a problem because wealthy people want to live in the old houses in Fes. | T | F |
| 5. The people in Fes don't want to lose their heritage. | T | F |

**C.** Watch the video again. Circle the correct answer.

1. The city of Fes was founded in the (ninth/eleventh) century.
2. By the 1300s, Fes was a center for (art/science) and learning.
3. (One or two/Five or six) families live in each house in the medina.
4. In the 18th-century palace, the first part that people bought was a (wall/fountain).
5. In the future, the Medersa will be a (museum/school).

## After You Watch

What are some important buildings and places in your city's heritage?
Make a list and then share the information with your partner.

_____

_____

_____

_____

_____

_____

_____

## Communication

Write a guide for foreign visitors to a historic place in your city.
Answer these questions in your guide.

1. Why should visitors go there?
2. What happened there?
3. What can visitors see and do there?
4. How much does it cost to visit? What hours is it open? How can visitors get there?

▲ the Pyramids at Giza, a popular tourist attraction

# THE BODY

1. What phrase best describes each picture?
   a. getting regular exercise
   b. eating plant foods
   c. maintaining social connections
   d. getting enough sleep

2. How do these activities keep people healthy?

## UNIT GOALS

Discuss ways to stay healthy
Talk about lifestyles
Suggest helpful natural remedies
Understand how germs affect the body

brain

artery

vein

bone

heart

lungs

liver

muscle

stomach

large intestine

small intestine

skin

## Vocabulary

**A.** Look at the picture. Then fill in the blanks below with the vocabulary words.

1. This pushes your **blood** through your body: _____
2. These carry blood around your body: _____ , _____
3. These bring air into your body: _____
4. This covers the outside of your body: _____
5. This makes your body move: _____
6. This lets you think and remember: _____
7. This does many different things: ___*liver*___
8. These digest food: _____ , _____ , _____
9. This supports your body: _____

Track 1-15

**B.** Listen and check (✓) the words you hear.

| | |
|---|---|
| ☐ **brain** | ☐ **stomach** |
| ☐ **large intestine** | ☐ **bone** |
| ☐ **heart** | ☐ **liver** |
| ☐ **artery** | ☐ **muscle** |
| ☐ **lungs** | ☐ **small intestine** |
| ☐ **vein** | ☐ **skin** |

## Grammar: Review of comparatives, superlatives, and equatives

| Comparatives | Superlatives | Equatives |
|---|---|---|
| The small intestine **is longer than** the large intestine. | The skin is **the** body's **largest** organ. | Your heart is **as large as** your fist. |
| *Comparative sentences express similarities or differences between two people or things. | *Superlative sentences express extremes among three or more people or things. | *Equative sentences are used when people or things are equal to each other. |
| *Form comparative sentences with -er + than or more/less than. | *Form superlative sentences with the + -est or the most/least. | *Form equative sentences with as + adjective + as |

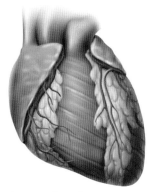

**human heart**

**human fist**

**A.** Complete the sentences. Use comparatives, superlatives, equatives, and the words in parentheses. In some sentences, more than one answer is possible.

1. Walking for exercise is _____ (good) than running.
2. Smoking is the _____ (bad) thing you can do to your lungs.
3. Green vegetables are the _____ (nutritious) kind of food for your brain.
4. Swimming is not the _____ (quick) way to build up your arm muscles.
5. Some elderly people are _____ (healthy) as some young people.

 **B.** Do you agree or disagree with the statements above? Use comparatives, superlatives, and equatives.

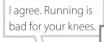

> I agree. Running is bad for your knees.

> But it's harder work, so maybe it's better for your heart.

## Conversation

Track 1-16

**A.** Close your book and listen to the conversation. Which body parts do the speakers mention?

**Ron:** What are you eating? It looks good.

**Valerie:** It's fish stew, and it is good! Did you know that eating fish is good for your brain?

**Ron:** Really? Is it good for anything else?

**Valerie:** Well, it's very **low in fat**, so it's good for your arteries, too.

**Ron:** And it's **high in protein**, right? So it could help you build muscles.

**Valerie:** Yes, I think you're right.

**Ron:** Hmmm. I just have a boring cheese sandwich.

**Valerie:** But cheese is full of calcium. That's good for your bones.

 **B.** Practice the conversation with a partner. Switch roles and practice it again. Then make a new conversation using foods you know about.

### Word Focus

Foods and drinks that are **high in X** or **low in X**, have a large or small amount of **X**. A food that's low in calories, for example, has a small number of calories.

✓ **Goal 1** **Discuss ways to stay healthy**

Talk with your partner about things you do to stay healthy.

> I try to avoid eating sugar.

> Good idea. I lift weights three times a week.

# Listening

 **A.** Discuss these questions with a partner. What determines how healthy you are? Are your **genes** or your **lifestyle** more important?

 **B.** Listen to three people talk about their health. Match the speaker to the correct picture.
Track 1-17

Speaker _____ Speaker _____ Speaker _____

| Word Focus |
| --- |
| **genes** = part of a cell that determines a person's physical characteristics (eye color, hair, intelligence, etc.) **lifestyle** = the manner in which we live |

**C.** Listen again and answer the questions.
Track 1-17

**Speaker A:**

1. What kind of exercise does Speaker A get? _____
2. Which family members does Speaker A mention? _____

**Speaker B:**

3. What kind of exercise does Speaker B get? _____
4. How often does Speaker B get sick? _____

**Speaker C:**

5. Why did Speaker C change her diet when she got older? _____
6. What do some people think about Speaker C's diet? _____

**D.** Work with a partner. Interview each other. Then tell the class about your partner's lifestyle. Find out about:

- Exercise: What kind? How often?
- Diet: What do you usually eat?
- Family History: Parents, grandparents, aunts, uncles, siblings.
- Stress: How much and what kind?

Ask other questions about lifestyle that you think are important.

# Pronunciation: Linking with comparatives and superlatives

> **Linking with comparatives and superlatives**
>
> When we use the comparative *-er* or *more*, and the next word starts with an /r/ sound, the words are linked together.
>
> When we use the superlative *-est* or *most*, and the next word starts with a /t/ sound, the words are linked together.
>
> She'll run in a longer race next month.     We had the best time of our lives.

Track 1-18

**A.** Listen to the sentences. Notice how the sounds are linked. Listen again and repeat the sentences.

1. It's a stricter religion than my religion.
2. This is the best tea for your stomach.
3. My grandfather is a faster runner than I am.
4. Which exercise is the most tiring?
5. You'll need a better reason than that.

 **B.** Underline the sounds that link together. Then read the sentences aloud to a partner.

1. This is the longest text message I've ever seen.
2. Today's news was more reassuring than yesterday's news.
3. What's the best time of the day for you to study?
4. Flower experts are trying to develop a redder rose.
5. He took the softest towel in the house.

## Communication

 What are the ingredients for an unhealthy lifestyle? Make a list with a partner of the worst things for your health. Then compare your list with the list of another pair of students.

> Not getting any exercise is the worst thing for your health.

> And worrying too much. That's really unhealthy.

 **Goal 2** **Talk about lifestyles**

> Talk to a partner. Who are the healthiest people you know? Compare their lifestyles with the lifestyles of the people from the listening section.

> **Engage!**
>
> Is your generation healthier or less healthy than your parents' generation?

# Language Expansion: Everyday ailments

For every common health problem, there's a product you can't live without. At least, that's what the advertisers want you to believe. For teenagers with **acne** or other skin problems, there's a miracle cream. A new shampoo will take care of the **dandruff** in your hair, and good old-fashioned aspirin will take care of your **headache** or **sore throat**. Are you suffering from **insomnia**? There's a pill to help you fall asleep. Did you eat the wrong kind of food, and now you have **indigestion**? There's a pill to end the burning feeling in your stomach. And if food won't stay in your stomach at all, take some medicine to take care of the **nausea**. Or maybe you ate too fast, and now you have the **hiccups**? Well, you won't find anything at the pharmacy for hiccups, but you can bet there's a company working on a new product right now.

**A.** Write the word in **blue** next to its definition.

1. _____ not able to sleep
2. _____ a skin condition of red spots, especially on the face
3. _____ a sharp sound you make in your throat
4. _____ a feeling like you are going to vomit
5. _____ dry skin that forms on the head and drops in little white pieces
6. _____ pain in the stomach because of something one has eaten
7. _____ a pain in your head
8. _____ a general feeling of pain in the throat

**B.** Read the article about natural remedies.

### A Natural Solution

Garlic for a cold? Chamomile tea for bad breath? These days, more and more people are turning to their grandparents' remedies to cure the minor illnesses and problems of everyday life. And why not? These natural remedies are usually safe, inexpensive, and, best of all, they work! (At least for some of the people, some of the time.) So the next time you're looking for a cure, skip the pharmacy and head to the grocery store for:

- **lemons** to stop the hiccups (Bite into a thick slice.)
- **ginger** to end nausea (Grind it and add hot water to make a tea.)
- **olive oil** to cure dandruff (Rub it into the scalp before shampooing.)
- **cucumbers** to reduce acne (Eat them often.)
- **onions** to relieve a headache (Put slices on your forehead, close your eyes, and relax.)

chamomile

garlic

lemon

olive oil

ginger

onion

cucumber

# Grammar: Infinitive of purpose

### Infinitive of purpose

You can drink tea with honey **to help** a sore throat.
I always use lotion with sunscreen **to protect** my skin.

*The infinitive of purpose gives a reason for doing something.
*It is formed with **to** + the base form of a verb.

 **C.** Match the actions with the reasons.

1. Get plenty of sleep at night ____
2. Eat fruits and vegetables ____
3. Take a nap ____
4. Give children warm milk ____
5. Ask your doctor questions ____
6. Lift weights ____

a. to help them fall asleep.
b. to find out the best remedy for your problem.
c. to increase your concentration during the day.
d. to make your muscles stronger.
e. to get enough vitamins in your diet.
f. to cure a headache.

## Conversation

Track 1-19

Track 1-19

**A.** Close your book and listen to the conversation. What remedies for tiredness do the speakers talk about?

**Olivia:**  Hi, Ashley. Are you drinking coffee? That's new.
**Ashley:**  Hi, Olivia. You're right. I usually don't drink coffee, but I need it today to wake up.
**Olivia:**  You do look tired. Did you get enough sleep last night?
**Ashley:**  No, I was worried about today's test, so it was hard to fall asleep.
**Olivia:**  Come on. Let's go for a walk.
**Ashley:**  Go for a walk? Why?
**Olivia:**  To wake you up and to get some oxygen to your brain before the test.
**Ashley:**  That's a good idea. Where do you want to go?

### Real Language

We say *That's new* when we notice something different or unusual.

 **B.** Practice the conversation with a partner. Switch roles and practice it again.

 **C.** Imagine that you or your partner has a health problem. Make a new conversation using your own ideas. Then role-play the conversation for the class.

## ✓ Goal 3   Suggest helpful natural remedies

Talk to a partner. What do you usually do to cure these common problems: a headache, bad breath, sore feet, and hiccups?

# Reading

**A.** Talk to a partner. Which of these can make you sick?

- shaking hands with someone
- being outside in cold weather
- eating food
- riding a crowded bus
- touching your eye
- playing a computer game

**B.** Circle **T** for *true* or **F** for *false*.

1. Viruses can only live inside people or animals.  T  F
2. All bacteria cause illnesses.  T  F
3. Washing your skin can prevent some illnesses.  T  F
4. Germs can enter the body through the eyes.  T  F
5. After they kill germs, antibodies stay in the body.  T  F
6. Vaccines kill germs in the body.  T  F

**C.** Tell a partner about the last time you got sick. How did you feel? Do you think your illness was caused by bacteria or a virus?

# Communication

Work in a small group. Make a list of serious illnesses that people in different parts of the world can get. How do people get those illnesses?

☐ The Human Body

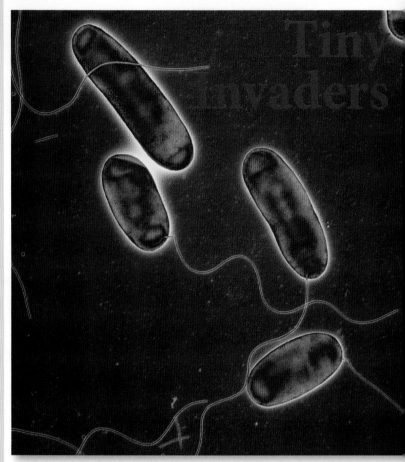

▲ Legionella bacteria

The human body is truly amazing. It allows us to sense the world around us, to do work and have fun, and to move from place to place. In fact, the human body does its work so well that most people don't think about it very much—until they get sick.

The germs that make people sick are everywhere. You can't see them, but they're there. They're sitting on your desk. They're hiding on your computer's keyboard. They're even in the air that you are breathing. There are two types of germs: viruses and bacteria. Viruses are germs that can only live inside animals or plants. Viruses cause illnesses such as the flu and measles. Bacteria are tiny creatures. Some bacteria are good. They can help your stomach break down food. Other bacteria aren't so good. They can make you sick. Bacteria can cause sore throats and ear infections.

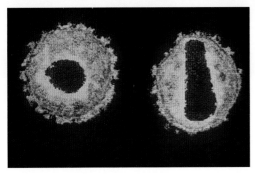

▲ HIV/AIDs virus

How can you stop these tiny invaders from making you sick? Your skin is the first defense against germs. You can prevent some illnesses simply by washing with soap and water. But germs can still enter the body through small cuts in the skin or through the mouth, eyes, and nose.

Once germs are inside your body, your immune system tries to protect you. It looks for and destroys germs. How does it do that? Special cells patrol your body. Some of these cells actually eat germs! Other cells make antibodies. An antibody sticks to a germ. There is a different antibody for each kind of germ. Some antibodies keep germs from making you sick. Others help your body find and kill germs. After a germ is destroyed, the antibodies stay in your body. They protect you if the same kind of germ comes back. That way you will not get the same illness twice.

You can keep your body healthy by eating a nutritious diet to make your immune system strong. You can also help your immune system fight germs by getting vaccinated. Vaccines are medicines. They contain germs that have been killed or weakened. The dead germs can't make you sick. Instead, they cause your body to make antibodies. If the same germ ever shows up again, then your antibodies attack it.

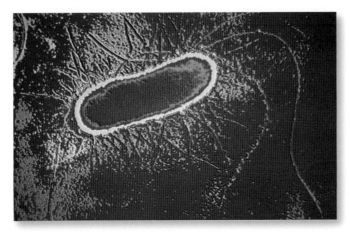

▲ E-coli

## Writing

Imagine you are a parent. Your child is sick and cannot go to school. Write a letter to your child's teacher to explain the situation.

_____
(date)

Dear (Mr./Ms.) _____,

_____

_____

_____

_____

_____

_____

_____

_____

_____

Sincerely,

_____

✓ **Goal 4** | **Understand how germs affect the body**

Talk to a partner. What happens when viruses or bacteria enter the body?

  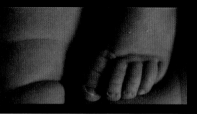 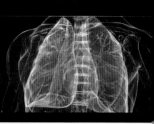

## Before You Watch

**A.** Brainstorm five things your body lets you do every day.

1. _____
2. _____
3. _____
4. _____
5. _____

**B.** Number the following 1 to 4, from smallest to largest.

_____ **organ**    _____ **cell**    _____ **organ system**    _____ **tissue**

## While You Watch

 **A.** Watch the video, *The Human Body*. Match the body's systems to the parts of the body or the cells they produce.

1. the circulatory system
2. the respiratory system
3. the digestive system
4. the nervous system
5. the reproductive system

a. the brain, spinal cord, and nerves
b. the heart
c. egg cells and sperm cells
d. the stomach and intestines
e. the lungs

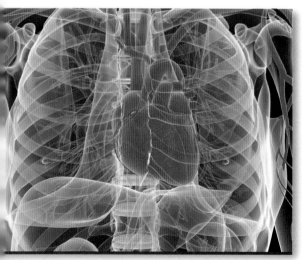

 **B.** Watch the video again. Circle **T** for *true* or **F** for *false*.

1. The heart is the body's strongest muscle.                T   F
2. Most nutrients enter the blood from
   the small intestine.                                      T   F
3. The brain is about the size of an orange.                 T   F
4. Another word for nerve cells is neurons.                  T   F
5. The human body begins as a single
   cell that divides.                                        T   F

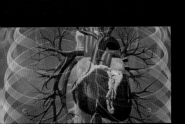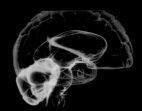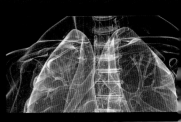

 **C.** Watch the video again. Write the numbers you hear.

1. Our hearts pump _____ gallons of blood each day.
2. Each of the _____ major organ systems in the human machine performs a special job.
3. The lungs pull in air, delivering oxygen as the air travels through _____ miles of airways.
4. Liquefied food travels into the small intestine, which can be over _____ feet long.
5. Neurons send signals rocketing through the brain at over _____ miles an hour.

## After You Watch

 What information from the video surprised you the most? What are some things you can do to take care of your body's systems?

## Communication

 You are in charge of designing a training program for an Olympic athlete. What will he or she eat every day? What kinds of exercise will he or she do, and how often? What else will help to get your athlete into top physical condition?

# CHALLENGES

1. What phrase best describes each picture?
   a. crossing the ocean in a sailboat
   b. walking in extreme heat or cold
   c. climbing a mountain
   d. learning a new skill

2. Look at the title of this unit. What do you
   think of when you hear the word *challenge*?

## UNIT GOALS

Talk about facing challenges
Reflect on past accomplishments
Use *too* and *enough* to talk about abilities
Describe a personal challenge

## Vocabulary

Track 1-20

**A.** Listen to part of a reality TV show and circle each word when you hear it.

| challenge | climb | cross | extreme | mental | physical | skill |
|---|---|---|---|---|---|---|

**B.** Read the paragraph. Fill in the blanks with the words in **blue**.

To me, learning to play a musical instrument is an **adventure**. You might feel afraid to try it, but it's as exciting as traveling to a new place, and the only **equipment** you need is a violin, a guitar, or in my case—an *oud*. When I started, my **goal** was to learn to play this **amazing** instrument well enough to play for my family. Now, I'm making good progress with the help of my music teacher. She thinks I'm getting better every week! I can probably **achieve** my goal soon, and then I'll play the *oud* at my parents' anniversary party.

1. When you have an _____ , you do something unusual and exciting.
2. A _____ is something you hope to be able to do through your efforts over time.
3. When you _____ something you succeed in making it happen.
4. The things you need for a particular activity are called _____ .
5. _____ means very surprising and wonderful.

## Grammar: Simple past tense vs. past continuous tense

| Simple past tense | Past continuous tense |
|---|---|
| I **called** you last night. | I **was studying** at the library last night. We **were eating** dinner *when you called*. |

*We use the simple past tense to talk about completed actions in the past.
*We use the past continuous tense to talk about things in progress at a specific time in the past.
*The specific time in the past is sometimes expressed with a time clause.

## Simple past tense with past continuous tense

| | |
|---|---|
| We **were practicing** our lines for the play *when* the lights **went out**. | She **looked** at the stars every night *while* she **was crossing** the ocean. |
| *When* the reporters **arrived**, Mr. Chen **was resting** on a bench. | *While* Roger **was climbing** the mountain, he **dropped** his water bottle. |

*To talk about an event in progress in the past that was interrupted, we can use a simple past time clause with *when* and a main clause in the past continuous tense.
*To talk about an event that was happening at the same time another event was in progress in the past, we can use a past continuous time clause with *while* and a main clause in the simple past tense.
*A comma is used when the time clause comes first in the sentence.

**A.** Complete the sentences. Use the past continuous form of the verb in parentheses.

1. William _____ (do) his homework when I arrived.
2. At three thirty I _____ (come) home on the bus.
3. The mountain climbers _____ (rest) when the storm began.
4. We practiced saying new vocabulary words while we _____ (walk).
5. You and your friends _____ (sit) in the coffee shop yesterday morning.

 **B.** Fill in the blank with *when* or *while*.

1. We were walking home _____ it started to rain.
2. Aki was studying for a test _____ her father walked in.
3. _____ he was walking, Adnan thought about his plans for the future.
4. Several buses went by _____ Mike and Laurie were sitting in the park.
5. _____ she got to her friend's house, people were talking and laughing.

## Conversation

Track 1-21

**A.** Close your book and listen to the conversation. What was Helen's biggest challenge last year?

> I called you last night, but you didn't answer your phone.

> I was studying at the library last night, so my phone was off.

| | |
|---|---|
| **Helen:** | What was the most difficult thing you did last year? |
| **Paul:** | Do you mean the worst thing? |
| **Helen:** | No, I mean your biggest challenge. |
| **Paul:** | Well, getting used to a new school when my family moved was difficult. |
| **Helen:** | For me, it was learning to play the saxophone. I'm still working on that! |
| **Paul:** | And you're making a lot of progress! |

 **B.** Practice the conversation with a partner. Switch roles and practice it again.

 **Goal 1** **Talk about facing challenges**

Talk with a partner. What challenges did you face last year? Use your own ideas.

## Listening

**A.** Which animals are **endangered**? Check (✓) the boxes.

☐ ▲ Madagascar giant jumping rat

☐ ▲ giant panda

☐ ▲ Siamese crocodile

☐ ▲ polar bear

☐ ▲ Antiguan racer (snake)

☐ ▲ African penguin

▲ Jenny Daltry, herpetologist and explorer

Track 1-22

**B.** Listen to the interview of Jenny Daltry. Circle the correct letter.
1. What amazing thing did Jenny Daltry do?
   a. She discovered a group of Siamese crocodiles.
   b. She found a new kind of bird in Cambodia.
   c. She helped scientists protect panda bears.
2. What was her biggest challenge?
   a. Walking through marshes.
   b. Avoiding dangerous snakes.
   c. Educating people about crocodiles.
3. How did she achieve her goal?
   a. She explained that crocodiles are important to the marshes.
   b. She explained that crocodiles are not really dangerous.
   c. She explained that crocodiles are extinct.

▲ marsh

Track 1-22

**C.** Listen again. Answer the questions.
1. How many crocodiles are in the largest group? _____
   _____
2. How many acres are now protected by the government? _____
   _____
3. How do most people feel about crocodiles? _____
   _____
4. What was Daltry doing when she found out about the Antiguan racer snake?
   _____

# Pronunciation: Words that end in -ed

Track 1-23

**A.** Listen to these words that end in -ed. The -ed is pronounced in three different ways.

| /t/ | /d/ | /ɪd/ |
|-----|-----|------|
| help   helped | listen   listened | start   started |

Track 1-24

**B.** Listen, repeat, and check the column of the sound you hear.

| Present tense | Simple past tense | -ed ending sound |||
|---------------|-------------------|------|------|------|
|               |                   | /t/ | /d/ | /ɪd/ |
| walk | walked | ___ | ___ | ___ |
| protect | protected | ___ | ___ | ___ |
| cross | crossed | ___ | ___ | ___ |
| discover | discovered | ___ | ___ | ___ |
| climb | climbed | ___ | ___ | ___ |
| start | started | ___ | ___ | ___ |
| need | needed | ___ | ___ | ___ |
| close | closed | ___ | ___ | ___ |

**C.** Say a word in the present tense. Ask your partner to say it in the past tense. Switch roles and practice it again.

# Communication

**A.** Work with a partner. Make a list of challenges people your age face.

**B.** Get together with another pair of students and compare your lists. Try to agree on the two or three most difficult challenges for people your age.

**Goal 2**  **Reflect on past accomplishments**

Tell a partner about someone famous or someone you know. What challenges did he or she face? How did this person achieve his or her goal?

**Word Focus**

To **achieve a goal** means to succeed in doing something you hoped to do.

▲ Subaru Takahashi, the youngest person to sail alone across the Pacific Ocean

## Language Expansion: Phrasal verbs

**A.** Read the article.

Subaru Takahashi was only 14 years old when he **set out** on an amazing adventure. His goal was to sail from Tokyo to San Francisco—alone. Subaru **grew up** near the sea, and loved sailing. His parents thought he was old enough to sail alone, and they helped him buy a boat. He left on July 22. At first, the trip was easy. Then after three weeks, his engine died, so he didn't have any lights. He had to **watch out** for big ships at night, because his boat was too dark to see. Five days later, his radio stopped working. Subaru was really alone then, but he didn't **give up**. His progress was very slow, but he **kept on** sailing. He almost **ran out of** food, and he was not fast enough to catch fish. He **put up with** hot sun and strong wind. On September 13, Subaru sailed into San Francisco. He was the youngest person ever to sail alone across the Pacific Ocean.

**B.** Match each phrasal verb from the article with its meaning.

1. set out ___
2. give up ___
3. watch out ___
4. grow up ___
5. keep on ___
6. run out of ___
7. put up with ___

a. accept something bad without being upset
b. grow from a child to an adult
c. finish the amount of something that you have
d. leave on a trip
e. be very careful
f. stop trying
g. continue trying

## Grammar: *Enough, not enough, too* + adjective

**A.** Read these sentences from the article and the questions that follow. Circle **Y** for *yes* and **N** for *no*.

1. *He was <u>old enough</u> to sail alone.*
   Could he sail alone?               Y      N

2. *He was <u>not fast enough</u> to catch fish.*
   Did he catch fish?                 Y      N

3. *His boat was <u>too dark</u> to see.*
   Could people see his boat?         Y      N

### Phrasal verbs

Phrasal verbs are two- or three-word combinations that have a special meaning. **set** + **out** = leave on a trip

### Engage!

What do you think about Subaru's parents? Was he really old enough to set out alone?

## Enough, not enough, too + adjective

| | |
|---|---|
| He was **old enough** to sail alone. | adjective + *enough* = You have the amount that you want. |
| He was **not fast enough** to catch fish. | *not* + adjective + *enough* = You don't have the amount that you want. |
| His boat was **too dark** to see. | *too* + adjective = It's more than the amount you want. |

**B.** Complete the sentences. Use *enough*, *not enough*, or *too* and the adjective in parentheses.

1. This boat is _____ (big) for one person.
2. It's _____ (expensive) for me to buy because I don't have much money.
3. It's _____ (strong) to sail in a lake.
4. It's _____ (safe) to sail in the ocean!
5. It's _____ (large) for a whole family.
6. Sailing is _____ (hard) for me to learn.
7. I'm _____ (afraid) to cross the ocean alone  because I can't swim.

# Conversation

Track 1-25

**A.** Close your book and listen to the conversation. What does Lisa need to do before she can climb the mountain?

**Lisa:** I want to climb Black Mountain next summer.

**Mari:** Are you serious? Black Mountain is too hard to climb. Don't you need special equipment?

**Lisa:** I already asked about it. I just need good boots.

**Mari:** And you're not strong enough to climb a mountain!

**Lisa:** You're right, I can't do it now. But I'll go hiking every weekend. Next summer, I'll be fit enough to climb the mountain.

**Mari:** Well, I like hiking. I'll go with you sometime!

 **B.** Practice the conversation with a partner. Switch roles and practice it again.

 **Goal 3**    **Use *too* and *enough* to talk about abilities**

Make new conversations about these things or amazing things you have done.

take a 100-mile bicycle trip          swim across Green Lake

Arctic Circle

# Arctic Dreams and Nightmares

## Reading

 **A.** What do you know about the Arctic? Circle the answers. Then read the article to check.

1. In the winter in the Arctic, it's dark ___ hours every day.
   a. 12
   b. 20
   c. 24
2. The North Pole is on ___.
   a. land
   b. water
   c. ice
3. In the Arctic, you can see ___.
   a. polar bears
   b. penguins
   c. polar bears and penguins

**B.** Answer the following questions. If necessary, look back at the article.

1. What was Boerge and Mike's idea?
   _____
2. What happened to their food?
   _____
3. How did Boerge and Mike travel?
   _____
4. How far did they go every day?
   _____
5. What happened when they were close to the Pole? _____
   _____
6. When did they get to the Pole?
   _____

▲ Ousland and Horn at North Pole

In the darkness of the Arctic night, a helicopter landed on the north coast of Russia. Boerge Ousland and Mike Horn were beginning one of the most amazing expeditions in history. It was January 22, and they planned to walk 600 miles (965 kilometers) to the North Pole—in winter.

There is no land at the North Pole, only ice that floats and moves. It's always a dangerous place, but winter is the worst. The sun doesn't come up for three months, and the temperature can be −40°F. But Boerge grew up in Norway, and he started skiing and climbing mountains as a boy. Mike Horn was a champion athlete from South Africa. They were ready for the challenge.

The two explorers wanted to set out right away, but the ice was moving too fast. They were waiting in their **tent** when Boerge heard a strange noise. "Mike, is that you?" Boerge asked. Suddenly, the tent ripped open. It was a polar bear! While they were looking for their gun, the bear grabbed some of their food. They didn't sleep very well that night.

The next day, they packed up their equipment and started their journey. They walked on skis, and pulled **sledges** behind them. The sledges could float on water and slide on snow. When the explorers came to open water, they had to swim. They put on waterproof suits over their clothes and got into the icy water, five or six times a day. When they weren't in the water, they were ski-walking. It wasn't light enough to see, so they used **headlamps.**

Every day, they skied and swam north. And while they were sleeping, the ice carried them south. But they kept on for 10 hours every day, covering 15 miles (24 kilometers) each day. They were getting close to the Pole when Mike became very ill. Blood was coming from his nose and ears. They had a cell phone, but Mike didn't want to give up and call for help. He took medicine from their **emergency kit,** and he slowly got stronger. And every day, the sky got a little bit lighter.

On March 23, Boerge checked his **GPS.** The North Pole was 1000 yards (914 meters) away. "I've been there before," Boerge told Mike. "You've never been. You go first."

"No," Mike said. "We'll do it together." And together, the two explorers walked to the Pole, and took this amazing photo.

**C.** Tell a partner about the expedition. What did they do? What problems did they have? In your opinion, what was the most amazing thing about the expedition?

# Writing

**A.** Complete the paragraph with the simple past or past continuous form of the verb in parentheses.

Last year, I _____ (decide) to run in the "Race for Life." It's a five-kilometer race that earns money for the city hospital. When I _____ (train) for the race, I _____ (get up) early every day. The first day, I _____ (run) for only two minutes, but I _____ (go) a little further every day. On the day of the race, I _____ (feel) great! I _____ (be) close to the end of the race when I _____ (fall) and I _____ (injure) my leg. So I _____ (walk) for the last kilometer. When I _____ (come) to the finish line, all my friends _____ (wait) for me there. I _____ (feel) very proud of meeting this challenge.

**B.** Write about your biggest challenge. Use another piece of paper. When did you face this challenge? What did you do? How did you feel after it?

✓ **Goal 4** | **Describe a personal challenge**

Tell a partner about your biggest personal challenge. Talk about the time, the place, what you did, and why it was difficult.

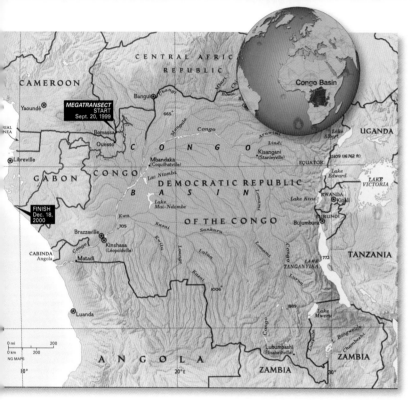

## Before You Watch

**A.** Read about the video. Check the meanings of the words in **bold**.

Dr. Michael Fay is a scientist with the Wildlife **Conservation** Society. He studies the **wildlife** of Africa, such as elephants and gorillas. He is beginning an expedition across the jungle of the Congo Basin. His goal is to count and record all of the animals in the **rainforest** before they **disappear**. He will face many challenges: crossing rivers, climbing mountains, and traveling through an area with no paths. Will he succeed?

**B.** List three things that you think Dr. Fay will do in the video.

1. _____

2. _____

3. _____

## While You Watch

**A.** Watch the video, *Megatransect Project*. Number the places in the order that you see them.

__ ocean      __ waterfalls      __ rainforest      __ river      __ hills

 **B.** Watch the video again. Circle **T** for *true* or **F** for *false*.

1. The Congo Basin has half of all kinds of the plants
   and animals in Africa.                                    T       F
2. Fay wanted to collect animals for a zoo.                  T       F
3. The expedition used boats to cross the waterfalls.        T       F
4. There are no other people in this part of Africa.         T       F
5. The expedition ended in a city.                           T       F

 **C.** Watch the video again. Write the numbers you hear.

1. how far they will walk: almost _____ kilometers
2. the size of the rainforest: over _____ square kilometers
3. how much of the world's rainforest is in the Congo Basin:
   one-_____
4. how far they can see on the hill: _____ or _____ kilometers
5. how much time they walked: _____ months

## After You Watch

 What do you think Dr. Fay's most difficult challenges were? Why?

## Communication

 **A.** You are going on an expedition to the African
rainforest. Make a list of the 10 most important
things to take with you.

**B.** Get together with another pair of students. Put
your lists from exercise **A** together and choose
10 items that your group will take.

**C.** Share your list with the class.

# TRANSITIONS

1. Have you done any of the things in the pictures? When?
   a. get married
   b. graduate
   c. have a child
   d. move

2. What are some other important transitions in life?

## UNIT GOALS

Use the simple past tense and past perfect tense to talk about milestones in your life

Talk about the best age to do something in your life

Use *how* questions to get more information

Describe an important transition in your life

## Vocabulary

**A.** Complete the photo captions with a phrase from the box.

| an adult    a baby    a senior citizen    a teenager    a child |

Infancy

He's _____ .

Childhood

He's _____ .

Adolescence

He's _____ .

Adulthood

She's _____ .

Old Age

He's _____ .

**B.** What do you think? At what age do people make these transitions?

1. from infancy to childhood _____
2. from childhood to adolescence _____
3. from adolescence to adulthood _____
4. from adulthood to old age _____

> A baby can't walk or talk.
> A child . . .

 **C.** Compare your answers in exercise **B** with a partner's answers. What changes take place in these transitions?

## Grammar: Simple past tense vs. present perfect tense

| Present perfect tense | Simple past tense |
|---|---|
| We use the present perfect tense: | We use the simple past tense: |
| *to talk about things that happened in the past—the specific time is not important.<br>*I've already **graduated** from college.* | *to talk about things that happened at a specific time in the past.<br>*I **graduated** in 2005.* |
| *to talk about things that started in the past and continue now.<br>*I've **lived** alone for five years now.* | *to talk about things that started and ended in the past.<br>*I **lived** alone for five years. Now I live with my wife and child.* |
| *to talk about things that happened several times in the past—the specific time is not important.<br>*I've **seen** that movie three times.* | |

**A.** Complete the sentences. Use the present perfect or simple past form of the verb in parentheses.

1. I _____ (live) in this apartment for five years. Before that, I _____ (live) with my parents.
2. The weather _____ (be) rainy yesterday. It _____ (be) rainy every day for a long time!
3. Hameed _____ (be, not) to North Africa, but he _____ (travel) in Jordan last year.
4. We _____ (start) this course two months ago. So far, we _____ (finish) five units.

**B.** Which of these things have you done? When did you do them for the first time? Write sentences with the present perfect tense or simple past tense.

1. fly

   _I've flown. I flew for the first time in 2003._  **OR**  _I haven't flown._

2. buy something very expensive

   _____

3. move out of your parents' house

   _____

4. find a gray hair on your head

   _____

5. get a drivers' license

   _____

 **C.** Compare your answers in exercise **B** with a partner's answers. At what stage of life do people usually do these things? At what age?

## Conversation

Track 1-26

**A.** Close your book and listen to the conversation. Where did Jason go?

| | |
|---|---|
| **Rick:** | Have you ever traveled alone? |
| **Jason:** | Yes, I have. It was fun! |
| **Rick:** | Really? Where did you go? |
| **Jason:** | I went to Los Angeles for a week last summer. |
| **Rick:** | Did you stay in a hotel? |
| **Jason:** | No, I visited my cousins. We had a great time. |

**B.** Practice the conversation with a partner. Switch roles and practice it again.

✔ **Goal 1**  **Use the simple past tense and past perfect tense to talk about milestones in your life**

Work with a partner. Take turns asking and answering questions about important moments in your life: during your infancy, your childhood, your adolescence, and your adulthood.

## Listening

 **A.** Discuss these questions.

1. Who is the oldest person you know? How old is he or she?
2. What does this person usually do every day?

 **B.** Listen to a radio program about Ushi Okushima, a woman from Okinawa, Japan. Answer the questions.

Track 1-27

1. Where does Ushi work? _____
2. Why is Ushi unusual? _____

 **C.** Listen again and find the information needed below.

Track 1-27

1. More than 700 people in Okinawa _____.
2. Three reasons for this:

   a. _____
   b. _____
   c. _____

3. Ushi's advice:

   a. _____
   b. _____
   c. _____

## Pronunciation: ə sound for unstressed vowels

**A.** Listen to the words. Notice the vowel sound of the unstressed syllables in **blue**. /ə/ is the symbol for this sound.

Track 1-28

**a**dult        childr**e**n        mill**io**n

**B.** Listen and repeat the words. Circle the unstressed syllables with the /ə/ sound.

Track 1-29

alone        license        person        banana        parents

paper        challenge        language        national        chicken

**Engage!**

Would you like to live to be 100? Explain your reasons.

# Conversation

**A.** Close your book and listen to the conversation. How old is Katie?

Track 1-30

**Andrea:** Did you hear the big news? Katie is getting married.
**Kim:** Seriously? But she's 17! That's much too young to get married.
**Andrea:** Oh, I don't know about that. She's known her boyfriend for a long time. And her family really likes him.
**Kim:** That's true . . . but I think she should wait a few years.
**Andrea:** Really? Well, what do you think is the best age to get married?
**Kim:** I think people should get married after they've finished college.

**Real Language**

You can say *Oh, I don't know about that* to disagree politely with someone.

**B.** Practice the conversation with a partner. Switch roles and practice it again.

**C.** Complete the chart with a partner. Use your own ideas. Then make new conversations about Kamal and Ali using the conversation in exercise **A** as an example.

| "Kamal is too old to change jobs." | "Ali is too young to get his own apartment." |
|---|---|
| Age:<br>Reasons why it's OK:<br><br>_____<br><br>_____<br><br>The best age for this is _____. | Age:<br>Reasons why it's OK:<br><br>_____<br><br>_____<br><br>The best age for this is _____. |

**D.** Read the opinions. How old do you think each person is?

1. "He's too old to play soccer."       Age: _____
2. "He's too young to travel alone."    Age: _____
3. "She's too old to work."             Age: _____
4. "He's too young to drive a car."     Age: _____
5. "She's too old to learn a new language."  Age: _____
6. "He's too old to get married."       Age: _____

## Goal 2   Talk about the best age to do something in your life

Compare your answers from exercise **D** with a partner's answers and explain your opinions. What is the best age for each of these things? Do you know someone who does these things at an unusual age?

## Language Expansion: Adjectives for age

**A.** Do you know someone who fits any of these descriptions? Who is it?

| | |
|---|---|
| **youthful** | older, but with the energy of a young person (good) |
| **childish** | older, but acting like a child (bad) |
| **elderly** | looking and acting old |
| **mature** | old enough to be responsible and make good decisions |
| **middle-aged** | not young or old (about 40–60) |
| **in his/ her twenties** | between 20 and 29 (also in his *teens, thirties, forties*, etc.) |
| **retired** | stopped working (often after 65) |

**B.** Talk about these people with a partner. How old are they? Describe them with adjectives from the box.

1.

2.

3.

4.

5.

6.

---

### Word Focus

**age** + **limit** = the oldest or **youngest** age that you can do something
**come** + **of** + **age** = become an adult

> I think she's in her teens, but she looks very mature.

---

## Grammar: *How* + adjective or adverb

### Questions with *how* + adjective or adverb

| | | | |
|---|---|---|---|
| **Adjectives** | He's very *tall*. | **How** tall is he? | About six feet. |
| **Adverbs** | He drives *fast*. | **How** fast does he drive? | Eighty miles an hour! |

*Use *how* to ask questions about descriptions with adverbs and adjectives.

**A.** Unscramble the questions.

1. English how do speak well you _____How well *do you speak English*_____ ?
2. you how are old _____ ?
3. can fast you how type _____ ?
4. you how tall are _____ ?
5. how do carefully write you _____ ?
6. how was hard exercise this _____ ?

**B.** Take turns with a partner asking the questions in exercise **A.**

**C.** Complete the conversations. Write questions using *how*.

1. **A:** I think Rita is too old to work full-time.
   **B:** Oh, I don't know about that. _____ ?
2. **A:** My brother failed his driver's license test six times because he drives so badly.
   **B:** Wow! _____ ?
3. **A:** I can't go to the game with you tonight, because my first class is very early tomorrow.
   **B:** That's too bad. _____ ?
4. **A:** I don't want to get my own apartment. It's much too expensive.
   **B:** Really? _____ ?
5. **A:** I haven't finished reading the assignment for tomorrow. I guess I read too slowly.
   **B:** That's a problem. _____ ?

## Conversation

Track 1-31

**A.** Close your book and listen to the conversation. What did Erik get?

**Mrs. Ryan:** My son Erik just got his first credit card.
**Mrs. Chen:** Do you think that's a good idea? He's just a college student!
**Mrs. Ryan:** That's true, but he has always been very careful with money.
**Mrs. Chen:** Really? How careful is he?
**Mrs. Ryan:** Well, in high school he had a part-time job. He saved enough money to buy a computer.
**Mrs. Chen:** Then maybe he is ready to get a credit card.

**B.** Practice the conversation in exercise **A** with a partner. Switch roles and practice again.

**C.** Look at these people and fill in ideas. Then make new conversations.

**Elizabeth**, in her 60s
started on a trip around
  the world
independent
reasons: _____
_____
_____

**Hameed**, 19
got his own apartment
mature
reasons: _____
_____
_____
_____

✓ **Goal 3** | **Use *how* questions to get more information**

Take turns with a partner giving a description of yourself or how you do something. Ask questions with *how* to get as much information as possible.

## Reading

 **A.** Discuss these questions with a partner.

1. At what age do people become adults?
2. How do you know when someone is an adult?

**B.** Read the article and answer the questions.

1. Where is the home of the Apache people?
   _____

2. What transition is the Apache Sunrise Ceremony about?
   _____

3. How long does the Sunrise Ceremony last?
   _____

4. How old was Nita when she had her Sunrise Ceremony?
   _____

5. Who helped her in the Sunrise Ceremony?
   _____

6. What did she wear?
   _____

7. How did she feel after the Sunrise Ceremony?
   _____

Southwestern United States

# Coming of Age the Apache Way

eagle feather

pendant

medicine man

massage

ground-up stones

The Apache Indians live in the southwestern region of the United States, and many of them still keep their traditional custom. A young Apache woman named Nita Quintero described one important custom:

The Sunrise Ceremony lasts for four days. It's the biggest ceremony of the Apache people—when a girl passes from childhood to womanhood. When my time came at 14, I didn't want to do it, because I felt shy. But my parents wanted it. My mother explained, "Then you will live strong to an old age." Older relatives and a **medicine man** helped us choose my sponsors, an older couple not related to us.

The ceremony started on Friday evening. One of my sponsors dressed me and put an **eagle feather** on my head and a shell **pendant** on my forehead. The dress is very special. It is made of soft leather, with 200 tiny bells. My mother and my aunt made it for me. For the rest of my life, I will wear this dress for special days. The most important thing that my sponsor did in the ceremony was to **massage** my whole body, to give me all her knowledge. Then I walked around the fire for many hours.

On Saturday, the medicine man sang to me in our Apache language. Even though it's my first language, I didn't understand all his words. After that, I ran for a long time so that bad people will never catch me. It started raining and my dress got very heavy, but I didn't feel tired.

The next day, one of my sponsors painted my dress and my skin with paint made from corn and four colors of **ground-up stones**. After the painting, my father poured corn and small candies over me, so that I will never be hungry in my life. Then he passed out many kinds of food to all the people to wish that they will always have lots of food. On Monday, the last day, there were more blessings and visiting with our family and friends. We gave everyone presents.

I'm really glad I had a Sunrise Ceremony. It makes me understand how much my parents care about me and want me to grow up right. Now my childhood is finished, and people know that I am a woman. If I have a daughter some day, I want her to have a Sunrise Ceremony, too.

▲ Nita Quintero dances for hours during the Sunrise Ceremony

**C.** Number the parts of the Sunrise Ceremony.

_1_ The family chooses two sponsors.

___ Her mother and aunt make a dress for the girl.

___ The girl runs.

___ The girl visits with her family and friends.

___ Her sponsor puts the dress on the girl.

___ Her sponsor massages the girl.

___ Her family gives people food.

___ Her sponsor paints the girl.

## Writing

Write a paragraph about a life transition. Be sure to include all of the following.

your age

what happened

how you felt before

how you felt after

why this transition was important in your life

**Goal 4** | **Describe an important transition in your life**

Talk to a partner about the important transition in your life that you wrote about above.

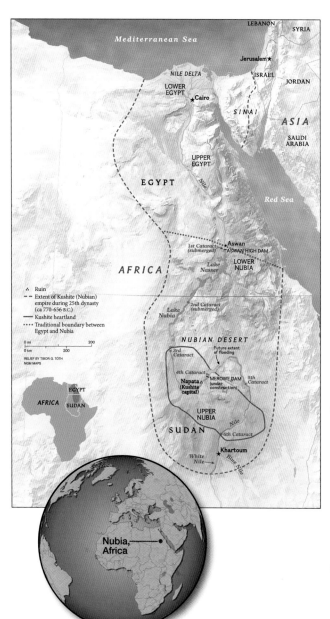

# Before You Watch

**A.** Talk with a partner about weddings that each of you has seen. Tell each other about these things:

**the bride   the groom     the ceremony     the celebrating**

How were the two weddings similar or different?

**B.** You are going to watch a video about a wedding in a Nubian village. Circle the word in each pair that you think will describe the wedding.

**short/long**

**modern/traditional**

**cheap/expensive**

**happy/sad**

# While You Watch

**A.** Watch the video, *Nubian Wedding*. Circle the things you see.

**white dress**

**wedding rings**

**wedding cake**

**dancing**

**B.** Watch the video again. Number the parts of the wedding in order.

_____ Everyone eats a special dinner.

_1_ The bride and groom sign special legal papers.

_____ The groom puts a ring on the bride's finger.

_____ The bride's skin is painted.

_____ The groom leaves his parents' house.

 **C.** Watch the video again. Answer the questions.

1. When did Sheriff meet Abir? _____
2. How many days does the wedding last? _____
3. When does the celebration start each day? _____
4. When did life change for the Nubians? _____
5. What do people eat at the wedding? _____
6. Who kisses the groom? _____

## After You Watch

 What surprised you the most about the Nubian wedding? How is it different from weddings in your country?

## Communication

Choose one of these life transitions and talk about gifts for a person who is celebrating it. With your group, make a gift guide with pictures and descriptions of five gift ideas for the person. Share your work with another group.

**getting your first job**

**having your first child**

**getting your first apartment**

**getting your driver's license**

**your own idea:** _____

# LUXURIES

1. Rank the luxury items from the pictures from the most desirable to the least.
   a. _____
   b. _____
   c. _____
   d. _____

2. Compare your list with a partner's list.

## UNIT GOALS

Explain how we get luxury items
Talk about needs and wants
Discuss what makes people's lives better
Evaluate the way advertising creates desire
   for products

fur coat

pearls

silk

precious metals

precious stones

jewelry

## Vocabulary

**A.** Write the word next to its definition.

1. smooth, round, white objects formed naturally in oysters _____
2. the material made by silkworms _____
3. extremely valuable, costly metals such as gold _____
4. a coat made from the hairy skin of an animal _____
5. extremely valuable, costly stones such as diamonds _____
6. decorative items that people wear like rings, bracelets, and necklaces _____

**B.** Think of three things your country imports and three things your country exports. Share your lists with the class.

| My country **imports** (buys from other countries) | My country **exports** (sells to other countries) |
| --- | --- |
| 1. | 1. |
| 2. | 2. |
| 3. | 3. |

## Grammar: Passive voice (present tense)

| Active voice | Passive voice |
| --- | --- |
| Subject + transitive verb + direct object | Direct object + *be* + past participle of transitive verb |
| Some people give jewelry as a gift.<br>My country imports cars from Italy.<br>Teens often wear designer jeans to school. | Jewelry **is given** as a gift (by some people).<br>Cars **are imported** from Italy (by my country).<br>Designer jeans **are** often **worn** to school (by teens). |

*Transitive verbs have direct objects.
*We use the passive voice with transitive verbs when the focus is on the object.
*The object goes before the verb in the passive voice.
*The passive voice is formed with the verb *be* plus the past participle of the main verb.
*Sometimes we use a *by* phrase with the passive voice.

**A.** Complete the sentences in the paragraph with the passive form of the verbs in parentheses.

Luxury items are expensive for a reason. Expensive watches, for example, _____ (make) from precious metals such as silver or platinum. Beautiful jewelry _____ (produce) by people, not by machines. Precious stones such as diamonds and opals _____ (separate) from tons of rock, and that requires expensive machinery. Imported luxury items _____ (bring) in from distant countries, so the cost of transportation adds to their expense. Finally, a luxury item such as perfume _____ (make) from special ingredients that can only be found in few places in the world.

**Word Focus**

**mined** = removed from the earth's surface

**B.** Match the luxury items to the actions.

1. Pearls ___
2. Animal skins ___
3. Diamonds ___
4. Perfume ___

a. are mined in several countries.
b. is worn on special occasions.
c. are found inside oysters.
d. are used to make fur coats.

 **C.** Take turns. Tell a partner about a luxury item you have or want to have. Where do you get it? How do you get it? How is it made?

# Conversation

**A.** Close your book and listen to the conversation. Who made Ellen's blouse?

Track 2-2

**Sandra:** That's a beautiful blouse! Is it silk?
**Ellen:** No, it's cotton, but it is soft like silk.
**Sandra:** I heard that the best cotton is grown in Egypt.
**Ellen:** Really? A lot of cotton is grown in India, too, but I don't know which kind is better.
**Sandra:** Where was your blouse made?
**Ellen:** In Sri Lanka. It was made by women in a co-op. They work together to make clothes. Then sell directly to the stores and keep the profit.
**Sandra:** That's great!

**B.** Practice the conversation with a partner. Switch roles and practice it again.

✓ **Goal 1** **Explain how we get luxury items**

Tell a partner about everything you're wearing today. Do you know who made your clothes and where they were made? Are you wearing anything imported? What are your clothes, jewelry, watch, perfume, or other things you're wearing made from?

## Listening

**A.** Match the activities with the pictures.

a. shopping for cut flowers at a street market

b. growing flowers in a greenhouse

c. packing colorful daisies in boxes

d. carrying roses at a wedding

**B.** Listen to three people talk about the cut-flower industry. Why is each country important to the flower industry?

Track 2-3

1. Japan ____
2. Ecuador ____
3. The Netherlands ____

a. has a good climate for growing flowers.
b. imports many flowers.
c. develops new kinds of flowers.

**C.** Listen again. Why is the flower industry important to each person?

Track 2-3

1. Shinobu: _____
2. Rafael: _____
3. Peter: _____

## Pronunciation: Sentence stress— content words vs. function words

In sentences, content words have specific meaning and receive greater stress. Other words have a grammatical function and receive less stress.

| Content Words | | | | |
|---|---|---|---|---|
| **nouns** | **main verbs** | **question words** | **adjectives** | **adverbs** |
| money | speak | why, where, how | wonderful | easily |

| Function Words | | |
|---|---|---|
| **pronouns** | **auxiliary verbs** | **the verb *be*** |
| it, she, him | have, is, will, could | is, are, was |
| **articles** | **prepositions** | **conjunctions** |
| the, a/n | in, to, of, at | and, or, but, so |

**A.** Listen to the stress in the following sentences. Then listen again and repeat.

Track 2-4

1. The <u>children</u> <u>listened</u> to a <u>story</u> about <u>pirates</u>.
2. Her <u>doctor</u> <u>lives</u> in an <u>enormous</u> <u>house</u>.
3. <u>Roses</u> and <u>carnations</u> are <u>popular</u> <u>kinds</u> of <u>flowers</u>.
4. <u>Gold</u> can be <u>mixed</u> with <u>copper</u> to <u>give</u> it a <u>red</u> <u>color</u>.
5. My <u>family</u> <u>needs</u> the <u>money</u> I <u>make</u>.
6. Have you <u>always</u> <u>wanted</u> to <u>move</u> to a <u>bigger</u> <u>city</u>?

**B.** Underline the content words. Then practice saying the sentences with a partner.

1. Flowers are an important part of life.
2. Delicious grapes can be grown in California.
3. I like diamonds and rubies, but they're very expensive.
4. My future could be very bright.
5. Celia wants to buy a new car.
6. Do you think she should get a small car?

# Communication

**A.** Write each item in the appropriate column. Use your own opinion.

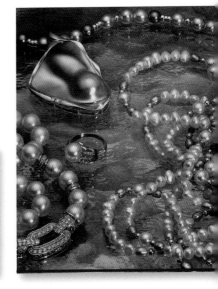

| a computer | a car | furniture | shoes |
| clean water | fresh fruit | books | flowers |
| money | a telephone | public parks | the Internet |

| Luxuries | Necessities |
| --- | --- |
|  |  |

 **B.** Compare your chart from exercise **A** with a partner's chart. Talk about why you think people need (or don't need) the items.

**Goal 2**  **Talk about needs and wants**

What is something you absolutely need? What luxury item do you want very much? Discuss these questions with a partner.

## Language Expansion: Past participles of irregular verbs

| | | |
|---|---|---|
| steal — stolen | fly — flown | spin — spun |
| dig — dug | spread — spread | mean — meant |

Fill in the blanks with the words in the box. Use your dictionary to help you.

1. Silk threads are _____ from silkworm cocoons.
2. Precious stones are _____ from the ground.
3. Fresh seafood can be _____ anywhere in the world in special coolers.
4. Salty caviar is _____ on a cracker and eaten.
5. Valuable paintings are sometimes _____ from art museums.
6. White roses are _____ as a symbol of purity.

## Grammar: Passive voice with *by*

**Passive voice with *by***

*The passive voice is usually used without a *by* phrase.
> Cut flowers **are sold** early in the morning.
> This watch **was made** in the 1920s.

*A *by* phrase is used when we want to say who or what does something (*the agent*).
> My rose **could be planted** by thousands of farmers.
> This blouse **was made** by well-paid workers.

**A.** Read the sentences and cross out the unimportant *by* phrases.

1. The Mercedes-Benz is made in Germany ~~by people~~.
2. This necklace was given to me by my grandmother.
3. King Tut's tomb was discovered by Howard Carter.
4. My car was stolen on April 19 by someone.
5. The company was founded by the owner's grandfather.
6. Even during the winter, daisies can be grown in greenhouses by workers.

**B.** Complete these sentences with a *by* phrase. Use your own ideas.

1. My favorite book was written by _____.
2. The clothes I'm wearing were made by _____.
3. My English class is taught by _____.
4. _____ was painted by _____.
5. _____ from my country is/are imported by_____.

**Word Focus**

**Necessities** are things we need such as food and shelter. **Luxuries** are things we don't really need, but they can be nice to have.

# Conversation

Track 2-5

**A.** Close your book and listen to the conversation. According to Gary, why is education valuable?

**Lance:** Gary, do you think people's lives are improved by money?

**Gary:** It depends. Some people don't have enough money to buy necessities. Their lives are definitely improved by having more money.

**Lance:** What about other people?

**Gary:** Well, when you have enough money for the basics, I think your life can be improved by education.

**Lance:** Interesting! Is your education improving your life?

**Gary:** Sure. I enjoy learning about new things, and I hope to get a good job someday because of my education.

**Lance:** I see what you mean. For me, though, my life would be improved by having a nice car.

**Gary:** OK, but nice cars cost money. Maybe you should think about getting a job first.

**Real Language**

We say *It depends* when we want to give an opinion that is not always true. We always mention the condition that makes it true.

 **B.** Practice the conversation with a partner. Switch roles and practice it again.

 **Goal 3** **Discuss what makes people's lives better**

Make new conversations. What do you think improves people's lives?

▲ This man is standing outside the Sephora perfume superstore in Paris.

## Reading

**A.** Discuss these questions with a partner.

1. Have you ever bought perfume or cologne? What brand did you buy?
2. Why do people wear perfume or cologne?
3. What do ads for perfume or cologne usually show?

---

**Word Focus**

**synthetic** = artificial, man-made
**renowned** = famous
**wilt** = If a flower wilts, it gradually turns soft and brown because it needs water or is dying.
**musk** = a substance with a strong smell that is used in making perfume
**gamble** = risk

---

Grasse, France

# Perfume: The Essence of Illusion

▲ "For me perfume is an indulgence," says Angie Battaglia, an Austin, Texas, businesswoman who owns 30 scents.

"Perfume," says Sophia Grojsman of International Flavors & Fragrances, "is a promise in a bottle." We want to believe. We want to be prettier, richer, sexier, and happier than we are. Consider the labels on the fragrances we buy: Joy, Dolce Vita, Pleasures, White Diamonds, Beautiful. Said Charles Revson, founder of the Revlon cosmetics company, "We sell hope."

In terms of chemistry, fragrances are a mixture of aromatic oils and alcohol. Perfume has a concentration of oils greater than 22 percent. Eau de parfum has a 15 to 22 percent concentration. The less aromatic eau de toilette has 8 to 15 percent oils, and cologne contains less than 5 percent oils. The "fixatives," or oils that make a fragrance last a long time, traditionally came from animals. Those have mostly been replaced by **synthetic** chemicals. The other ingredients came from plants, most notably flowers.

The area around Grasse, France, is **renowned** for its flower plantations. Farmers like Joseph Mul have been producing roses, jasmine, and lavender for centuries. Mul's rose absolute, a liquid extracted from rose petals, sells for $3650 a pound. Explains Mul, "Picking roses will never be done by machine." The rose petals are carefully harvested by hand during the early morning. By ten o'clock, the heat of the sun begins to **wilt** the flowers, and the workers are done for the day. "Labor is 60 percent of the cost," says Mul.

The high cost of natural ingredients is just one of the reasons that perfumers today also use artificial ingredients in their fragrances. Synthetics also allow perfumers to use scents such as lilac that cannot be obtained naturally, or scents from flowers that are too rare to be picked. Synthetics save wild animals from being used for their **musk** as well. According to perfumer Harry Fremont, "Good fragrance is a balance between naturals and synthetics."

Once perfumers have created a lovely fragrance, it's time for the marketing department to work its magic. The industry spends hundreds of millions of dollars each year to convince people to buy something they don't really need. The success rate for new perfumes is low—only about one in ten is successful, so spending money on advertising is a big **gamble**. It's also the only way to let the world know about a fragrance so enchanting that it can make us believe our dreams will come true.

▲ A woman picks night-blooming jasmine flowers at dawn in a field in India.

 **B.** Write answers to the questions.

1. What are the two main ingredients in perfume? _____
2. Why do perfume makers use fixatives? _____
3. Which French city is famous for its flower farms? _____
4. What are the four advantages of synthetics? _____
5. What percentage of new perfumes succeed? _____

**C.** Make a list of other products designed to make people feel better about themselves. Share your list with the class and talk about whether the products really do what they're supposed to do.

# Writing

**A.** Create a magazine ad for a new perfume for men or for women. You will need to:

• Give the perfume a name.
• Draw a simple picture or cut out magazine photographs to illustrate your ad.
• Write a few sentences about the perfume.

**B.** When you're finished, present your ad to the class.

**Goal 4** | **Evaluate the way advertising creates desire for products**

Choose a luxury item and talk with a partner about the way it is marketed. What forms of advertising are used? How do the advertisers "convince people to buy something they don't really need"?

Southern
Australia,
Australia

# Before You Watch

**A.** Read the sentences. Write each word in **blue** next to its definition.

1. The **ground** under Coober Pedy, Australia, contains beautiful stones called opals.
2. **Digging** is one thing you can do in the ground.
3. The Australian **outback** is generally very dry and hot.
4. Very beautiful opals can be worth a **fortune**.
5. Everyone in Coober Pedy hopes for a big **payoff** for all their hard work.
   a. _____ the parts of Australia that are far away from cities
   b. _____ a large sum of money
   c. _____ the earth, soil
   d. _____ the benefit you get from an action
   e. _____ to make a hole by taking away earth

**B.** Tell your partner about your idea of a *treasure*. What is so valuable to you that you would spend your life working to get it?

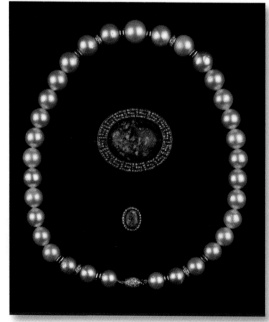

▲ Opal jewelry surrounded by a string of pearls

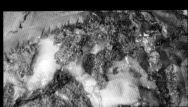

## While You Watch

**Word Focus**

**miners** = people who dig for stones or other minerals

 **A.** Watch the video, *Coober Pedy Opals*. Circle each word when you hear it.

| digging   fortune   outback   payoff   ground |

 **B.** Watch the video again. Circle **T** for *true* or **F** for *false*.

1. About three thousand people live in Coober Pedy.   T   F
2. Over eighty percent of all opals come from Australia.   T   F
3. Ninety-five percent of all opal is colorless.   T   F
4. The hope of a huge payoff motivates people to dig for opals.   T   F
5. Most people in Coober Pedy make a fortune eventually.   T   F

 **C.** Watch the video again. Write your opinions.

1. Is finding opals a scientific process? Why? _____
   _____
   _____

2. Why does the video talk so much about *hope*? _____
   _____
   _____

3. Do people have a high quality of life in Coober Pedy? Why?
   _____
   _____
   _____

## After You Watch

Some of the holes and tunnels in Coober Pedy are later converted into homes. What might be the advantages and disadvantages of living in these underground homes?

## Communication

Imagine that Coober Pedy doesn't have enough miners. Create a newspaper or Internet job listing for opal miners. Describe the work and the potential rewards. Try to attract new people to Coober Pedy!

▲ (top) Coober Pedy
(bottom) underground house

# NATURE

1. What animals are these? Where do they usually live?

2. In what ways are these animals similar? How are they different?

## UNIT GOALS

Use conditionals to talk about real situations
Talk about possible future situations
Describe what animals do
Give your opinion about a problem in nature

## Vocabulary

**A.** Read the sign. Notice the words in **blue**.

> **Asiatic Black Bear** (*Ursus thibetanus*)
>
> This is an Asiatic black bear. It's one of eight different **species** of bears. Its **habitat** is the forests of northern Asia. These bears are **predators** that eat other animals. Their usual **prey** is small animals and fish. They **hunt** for their food during the day. The bear in our zoo is **wild** and came from a forest in China. In the past, some other kinds of **tame** bears performed in shows. Asiatic black bears are endangered, and there are only a few of them left. People kill them to use their body parts in traditional medicine. If we don't **protect** these bears, they will be **extinct** a few years from now. We must all do our part to save the world's **wildlife**.

Range of Asian black bear
(*Ursus thibetanus*)

NG MAPS

**B.** Write the words in **blue** next to the correct meanings.

1. to look for animals and kill them _____
2. an animal that other animals kill to eat _____
3. an animal that kills other animals _____
4. the place where an animal usually lives _____
5. a kind of animal _____
6. doesn't exist any more, all dead _____
7. animals and plants that live in nature _____
8. to keep safe from danger _____
9. in nature, not controlled by people _____
10. trained to live with people _____

## Grammar: Real conditionals in the future

**A.** Study the sentence and answer the questions.

   Condition                     Result

**If we don't protect these bears, they will be extinct a few years from now.**

1. Is the condition possible, or not possible? _____
2. Is the result now, or in the future? _____

### Real conditionals in the future

| Condition | Result |
|---|---|
| *if* + subject + present tense verb | subject + *will* + verb |
| **If** I have time tomorrow, | I'**ll** call you. |
| **If** we don't protect Asiatic black bears, | they **will** be extinct a few years from now. |

*These sentences tell about situations in the future that are possible.
*The clause with *if* can be at the beginning or the end of the sentence.

**B.** Complete the sentence with the correct form of the verb in parentheses.

1. If an elephant _____ (live) in a zoo, it _____ (get) bored.
2. We _____ (be) very happy if our team _____ (win) the game.
3. If I _____ (see) a bear in the forest, I _____ (run) away.
4. I _____ (go) to the match if I _____ (have) enough money for a ticket.
5. If you _____ (sleep, not) enough, you _____ (feel) tired tomorrow.

 **C.** Discuss these situations with a partner. Write sentences to describe them. What will happen if . . .

1. Asiatic black bears can't find enough food?_____
   _____

2. people cut down the forests in Asia? _____
   _____

3. people use more traditional medicine? _____
   _____

4. people protect Asiatic black bears?
   _____

**Real Language**

You can say *That may be, but . . .* to show that you disagree with the other person's idea.

## Conversation

Track 2-6

**A.** Close your book and listen to the conversation. What is Katie afraid of?

**Mike:** Let's go camping in the national park.
**Katie:** I'm not sure that's a good idea. There are bears in the park.
**Mike:** That may be, but they're not very big. And they stay away from people.
**Katie:** If I see a bear, I'll be really scared. They're so dangerous!
**Mike:** Bears won't hurt you if you leave them alone.

**B.** Practice the conversation with a partner. Switch roles and practice it again.

**C.** Make two new conversations.

1. White Beach/sharks
2. your own idea _____

 **Goal 1** | **Use conditionals to talk about real situations**

Talk to your partner about situations that will affect nature.

## Listening

**A.** Look at the map and label these places.

| Atlantic Ocean | Pacific Ocean | Indian Ocean | Mediterranean Sea |

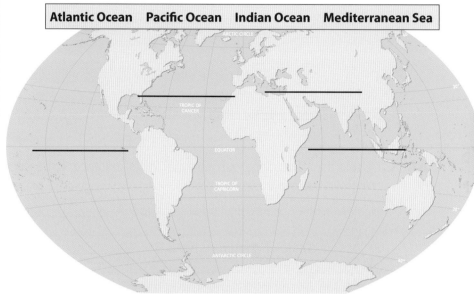

 **B.** Listen to the radio program about the bluefin tuna and circle the three places it talks about.
Track 2-7

 **C.** Listen to the first part of the radio program again. Use the information to fill in the blanks.
Track 2-8

**Bluefin Tuna**
1. Up to _____ feet long
2. Weighs more than _____
3. Colors: _____, _____, _____
4. Swims more than _____ miles an hour
5. Lives up to _____ years

▲ These bluefin tuna from a fish farm in the Mediterranean will become sushi in Japanese restaurants.

 **D.** Listen to the second part of the program again and complete the sentences.
Track 2-9

1. In _____ people use it to make sushi, and in _____, people love to cook big pieces for tuna steaks.
2. If the boats _____ big bluefins, there _____ young fish in the future.
3. Only _____ of the original population of bluefins was left.
4. If the big boats _____ the fishing in the Mediterranean, many poor people _____ their jobs.
5. If this amazing fish _____, the seas _____ a great treasure.

 **E.** Discuss these questions with a partner.

1. Is fish cheap or expensive where you live? How often do you eat it?
2. Do you know where your fish comes from?

## Pronunciation: Phrases in sentences

**A.** Listen and repeat these sentences. Notice how they're divided into phrases.

Track 2-10

1. A bluefin tuna | can swim very fast | and live a long time.
2. My friend's birthday | is June fourteenth.

**B.** Divide these sentences into phrases.

1. Jeff and I saw three big sharks.
2. Cathy doesn't like dogs or cats.
3. I'll bring my camera if we go to the zoo.
4. How many children do you have?
5. My friends and I go out dancing every Saturday night.

**C.** Listen and check your answers. Then take turns saying the sentences to your partner.

Track 2-11

## Communication

**A.** Read the information. What does *sustainable* mean?

Fish is one of the world's favorite foods. Around the world, the average person eats 36 pounds (16 kg) of fish every year. But many kinds of fish around the world are disappearing because people catch too many of them. Scientists say that 90 percent of the biggest fish are gone now. If we catch too many big fish now, there won't be any baby fish in the future. Our way of fishing now is not **sustainable**— it can't continue for a long time without hurting the environment.

 **B.** You are members of an environmental group called **Save the Oceans**. Your group wants to take action to solve the fishing problem, and it is thinking about three different plans. Talk about these plans. What will happen if we follow each one?

> **Plan A: Don't eat fish!**
> Tell people to stop buying and eating fish. Put ads in newspapers and magazines, and make TV commercials to explain why fishing hurts the environment.
>
> **Plan B: Safe fish symbol**
> Make a special symbol for fish that is caught in a sustainable way. Make commercials to tell people to look for this symbol in supermarkets and restaurants.
>
> **Plan C: Strict laws about fishing**
> Make stronger laws about how many fish people can catch. Send special police in fast boats to all of the fishing areas to make sure that fishing boats follow the laws.

 **Goal 2** **Talk about possible future situations**

Which is the best plan? Why? Explain your decision to the class.

## Language Expansion: Adverbs of manner

**A.** How do they do it? Look at the pictures. Complete the sentences with an adverb from the box.

| beautifully | fast | well | slowly | loudly | badly |
|---|---|---|---|---|---|

1. A snail moves _____*slowly*_____.
2. A cat hunts _____.
3. A penguin walks _____.
4. A shark swims _____.
5. A lion roars _____.
6. A bird sings _____.

### Adverbs of manner

| Adjective + *ly* | | Irregular adverbs | |
|---|---|---|---|
| quick + *ly* = **quickly** | | good | **well** |
| careful + *ly* = **carefully** | | fast | **fast** |
| happy + *i* + *ly* = **happily** | | hard | **hard** |

*Adverbs of manner tell how an action is done.
  A snail moves **slowly**.
  A cheetah runs **fast**.

*Adverbs of manner come after the verb.

**B.** What is the adverb for each adjective? On another sheet of paper, write a sentence using the adverb.

| quick | careful | quiet | easy | loud |
|---|---|---|---|---|

## Grammar: Review of quantifiers

**A.** Read about raccoons and the things they eat. Work with a partner to decide if their foods are count or non-count nouns.

Raccoons are small animals that live in North America and some parts of Europe. They are *omnivores*—animals that eat both plants and animals. A raccoon's usual food is nuts and fruit. They also like to eat insects. They climb in trees to eat bird eggs. Sometimes, they also catch fish or frogs. Some raccoons live in cities. They cause problems there because they like to eat garbage. They look for things like meat, bread, and potatoes in people's garbage cans. They'll even eat soap if they find it!

**B.** Review the information in the chart. Then circle the correct quantifier in each sentence below.

| Quantifiers | | | |
|---|---|---|---|
| **With count nouns** | | **With non-count nouns** | |
| too few<br>a few<br>some<br>a lot of<br>many<br>too many | eggs | too little<br>a little<br>some<br>a lot of<br>too much | meat |

*Quantifiers tell us *how much* or *how many*.
*Don't use *much* in affirmative sentences: ~~He has much money.~~ He has a lot of money.

1. Raccoons eat (many/a little) different kinds of food.
2. They eat (a little/a lot of) nuts
3. Raccoons will eat (a few/a little) insects if they find them.
4. They sometimes eat (a little/many) soap.
5. If a raccoon goes in your garbage can, you'll find (a lot of/many) garbage all around the place!

## Conversation

Track 2-12

**A.** Listen to the conversation with your book closed. What does the woman want to see at the zoo?

| | |
|---|---|
| **Dan:** | So, which animals do you want to see at the zoo? |
| **Carmen:** | I love to look at the penguins. I think they're really amazing. |
| **Dan:** | Why is that? |
| **Carmen:** | Well, they walk so slowly, but in the water they swim really well. And it's fun to watch them at feeding time. |
| **Dan:** | Really? What do they eat? |
| **Carmen:** | They eat a lot of fish and a few shrimp. |

**B.** Practice the conversation with a partner. Switch roles and practice it again.

**C.** Fill in the chart. Add your own ideas. Then make new conversations.

| bread   walk   play   leaves   grass   climb   run   bananas |
|---|

| | What it does | What it eats |
|---|---|---|
| 1. camels | | |
| 2. monkeys | | |

✓ **Goal 3**  **Describe what animals do**

Report to the class. Tell them about your favorite zoo animal.

## Reading

**A.** Discuss these questions with a partner.

1. Why do people visit national parks and other nature areas?
2. What are the most famous nature areas in your country? What problems do they have?

**B.** Circle **T** for *true*, **F** for *false*, or **NI** for *no information* (if the answer is not in the reading).

1. There are no wolves in Yellowstone today.　T　F　NI
2. Wolves can kill animals that are much bigger than them.　T　F　NI
3. Wolves live in families.　T　F　NI
4. Wolves often hurt people.　T　F　NI
5. People killed all of the wolves in Yellowstone.　T　F　NI
6. Wolves sometimes kill farm animals.　T　F　NI
7. Wolves can run very fast.　T　F　NI

**C.** Number the events to put them in order.

**a.**
____ There are fewer elk.
____ More willow trees grow.
____ The wolves kill and eat elk.
____ There are more wolves in the park.

**b.**
____ The wolves get out of the park.
____ The wolves kill cows and sheep.
____ Ranchers lose money.
____ Ranchers get angry.

Yellowstone National Park, United States

# Return of the Gray Wolf

eagle

bighorn sheep

bison

elk

Yellowstone National Park in the United States is one of the most beautiful places in the world. In the park, visitors see many kinds of wildlife like **bison**, **elk**, and **bighorn sheep** in their natural environment. But for many years, one animal was missing: the gra wolf. These wolves still lived in Canada, but they were disappearir in the United States.

Wolves are very intelligent animals. They learn, play, and live families—the same way dogs do. They communicate with the othe wolves in their pack, or family, with their voices. They kill their pr with their sharp teeth. When wolves are together in their packs, t hunt very large animals like bison.

Starting in the 1800s, people hunted gray wolves in Yellowsto because they were dangerous predators. In 1926, the last wolf in t park was killed. But some scientists thought that this was bad for ecosystem. If there are no predators, the population of prey anim gets too large. In 1976, the government made it illegal to kill wolves. And in 1995, scientists started a new program. They brought 31 wolves from Canada to live in Yellowstone.

Some people were very angry about this program. Tourists were afraid of wolf attacks, though wolves don't usually hurt people. Ranch owners don't like wolves because they kill their sheep and cows. In the first few years, wolves killed 80 sheep and 5 cows near the park. Scientists say that was only a few animals, but ranchers say it was too many.

The wolves in Yellowstone have helped the park's ecology. If wolves kill an elk, they will leave a lot of meat for other animals, because an elk is too big for wolves to eat completely. So the wolves give food to animals and birds like **eagles**. The wolves also helped the trees. If there are no wolves, there will be too many elk. The elk won't have enough food, so they eat small willow trees and kill some kinds of forests. After the wolves came back to the park, they killed and ate the elk, and the willow trees started to grow again.

Today, there are more than 1,000 gray wolves around Yellowstone. And once again, you can hear their voices at night.

NGM MAPS

# Communication

**A.** Choose a role. Make notes on your opinions about wolves.

> 1. You are a rancher near Yellowstone National Park. Gray wolves have killed five of your sheep. You can sell your sheep for $500 each.

> 2. You are a travel company owner. You take visitors on tours to Yellowstone National Park. They sleep in tents and take photos of the wildlife.

> 3. You are a scientist who studies wolves. You want to find out how young wolves learn to hunt.

**B.** The government wants to bring more wolves to Yellowstone. Role play a meeting of the three people described in exercise **A.**

# Writing

Should the government help dangerous animals? Write a paragraph about your opinion.

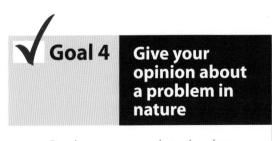

✓ **Goal 4** **Give your opinion about a problem in nature**

Read your paragraph to the class.

## Before You Watch

 Read about the video and check the meanings of the words in **bold**.

> Elephants are beautiful and intelligent animals. They can use their **trunks** to pick up heavy things. **In the wild**, they live in **herds** in the forest. Today, many elephants live in zoos or circuses. Their **trainers** take care of them and try to make a good life for them. But can elephants be happy **in captivity**?

## While You Watch

 **A.** Watch the video, *Happy Elephants*. Choose the main idea.

1. Elephants are happier in the wild.
2. People and elephants have been together for a long time.
3. Elephant trainers find ways to make elephants happier.

 **B.** Watch the video again. Circle the things that elephants like.

swimming    living alone    people talking to them    mud    living in a new place

 **C.** Watch the video again. Fill in the information.

1. Elephants and people have worked together for over _____ years.
2. There is one question that people have been asking: How is it possible to keep elephants happy _____ ?
3. Many people who work closely with animals say that they do have _____ and can experience happiness.
4. That means that they live in families and herds and they _____ other elephants.
5. For elephants, communication and social relationships are really _____ .
6. This communication and pleasant activity makes everyone _____ .

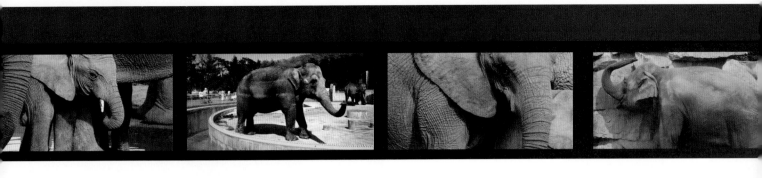

## After You Watch

 Discuss these questions with your partner.

1. Have you visited a zoo, or seen a video of a zoo?
2. Do you think the animals like living there? Why, or why not?

## Communication

 You are the directors of a new zoo in your country. Choose one kind of animal that you will display in the zoo, and plan a home for these animals. Think about how the animal lives and what it likes. Also think about how you will help visitors understand the animal. Draw a plan for the animal house. Share your plan with another group.

# LIFE IN THE PAST

1. How has life changed over the past 500 years? Talk about these things:
   a. travel
   b. chores
   c. clothing
   d. communication
2. Which of these changes are the most important to you?

## UNIT GOALS

Discuss life in the past
Talk about your grandparents' daily lives
Compare past and present ways of getting things done
Consider the impact of the Columbian Exchange

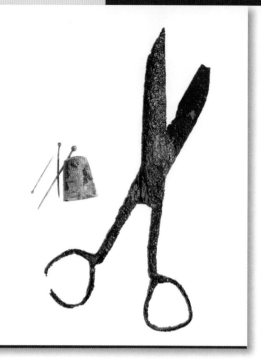

▲ Pins, thimble, and scissors found at Jamestown Colony excavation

## Vocabulary

Track 2-13

**A.** Listen to part of a TV documentary and circle each word when you hear it.

| | | |
|---|---|---|
| tools | weapons | hunting |
| pipes | combs | glass beads |
| building | hairbrushes | farming |

**B.** Complete the sentences with words from the box.

1. Less than 500 years ago many people used simple _____ and _____ to do their own _____, _____, and _____.
2. Women would use simple _____ and _____ made from wood or bone.
3. Men used to smoke tobacco in _____.
4. _____ were worn as jewelry.

Track 2-13
**C.** Listen again to check your answers.

### Real Language

We say that we *take something for granted* when we think of it as normal and do not think about it.

## Grammar: *Used to* and *would*

| Used to | Would |
|---|---|
| Native Americans **used to** make their own shoes out of deerskin. (Now, most of them don't.) | When early Indian hunters wanted to hunt ducks, they **would** make duck decoys—artificial ducks to attract the real ones. |
| They **didn't use to** buy their shoes at a store. (Now, most of them do.) | **Would** people buy or make their everyday tools? |
| **Did** you **use to** take music lessons? | |

*We use *used to* (or *didn't use to*) to talk about past situations or habitual actions in the past that are not true now.
*In negative statements and questions with *used to*, the auxiliary *did* or *didn't* shows the past tense and *use* is in the base form. (There is no significant difference in the pronunciation of *used to* and *use to*.)
*We sometimes use *would* in the same way.
*We usually don't use the negative *wouldn't* in this way.

**A.** Complete each sentence with *used to* or *would*. (Both forms are possible.)

### Six Indian Innovations

| | |
|---|---|
| **chewing gum** | • The Aztecs _____ chew chicle, a latex from the sapodilla tree and the key ingredient in modern chewing gum. |
| **popcorn** | • Native Americans made the first popcorn. Some Indians _____ put a stick through a dried corn cob and hold it over a fire. |
| **parkas** | • Today's ski jackets are similar to hooded coats Inuit women _____ make from layers of skins that trapped air for greater insulation. |
| **sunglasses** | • The Inuit also _____ carve their version of sunglasses from walrus tusks with narrow slits for people to look through. |
| **chocolate** | • The Maya created the first chocolate from cacao beans. The Maya, Toltec, and Aztec Indians _____ drink a bitter, unsweetened mixture. Sugar was added later to suit European tastes. |
| **dental care** | • North American Indians _____ scrub their teeth with the ragged ends of sticks, while the Aztec Indians applied salt and charcoal to their teeth. |

**B.** Talk about the innovations in exercise **A.** Which ones did you already know about? Which ones surprised you? Use *used to* and *would*.

I already knew the Maya **used to** make a chocolate drink.

Me, too, but I'm surprised Native Americans **would** use syringes.

## Conversation

**A.** Close your book and listen to the conversation. Why are the Incan ruins amazing?

Track 2-14

**Ben:** What's up, Patricia?
**Patricia:** Not much. I'm looking at pictures of Incan ruins in Peru.
**Ben:** Wow, they used to cut a lot of huge stones! How did they do it?
**Patricia:** They would use tools made of stone or bronze, but the stones are cut and placed so accurately that even modern people are amazed.
**Ben:** And how did they get the stones up the Andes mountains?
**Patricia:** Actually, the Inca used to get their stones from the area where they were building.

**B.** Practice the conversation with a partner. Switch roles and practice it again.

✔ **Goal 1**  **Discuss life in the past**

Talk with a partner about early civilizations in your country.
What were their lives like?

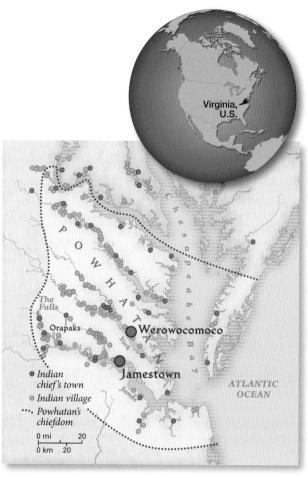

## Listening

**A.** What did European colonists take to the New World? Check the items you think might have been found in a recent archaeological dig. Add your own ideas.

- ☐ tools for farming
- ☐ pipes for smoking tobacco
- ☐ glass beads
- ☐ hairbrushes and combs
- ☐ iron nails for building
- ☐ weapons
- ☐ _____
- ☐ _____

**B.** Listen to an interview with an archaeologist. Which of the items from exercise **A** does he mention?

Track 2-15

**C.** Listen again and answer the questions.

Track 2-15

1. What did archaeologists NOT use to know about the Jamestown Colony?

_____

_____

2. Why did some of the colonists bring dice to the Jamestown Colony?

_____

_____

3. What kinds of clothes did the archaeologists find? _____

_____

4. When was tobacco introduced to Europe? _____

_____

5. What did the colonists bring that the Indians especially valued? _____

_____

**D.** Work in pairs. Imagine that you and your partner are going to spend a month in a wilderness area. You will not be able to communicate with the outside world or buy anything there. Make a list of the 12 things you will bring with you.

**Engage!**

Do you think it's important to study the past? Or do you think we should focus more on the future? Give your reasons.

# Pronunciation: Reduction of *used to*

When we speak quickly, *used to* is sometimes pronounced *YOU-sta*.

Track 2-16

**A.** You will hear each sentence twice. Listen to the full form and the reduced form of *used to*. Listen again and repeat the sentences.

1. People used to make their own tools.
2. They used to plant corn here.
3. Did you use to play baseball?
4. Food used to cost a lot less.
5. My grandfather used to read to me.

**B.** Complete the sentences with your own information. Then read the sentences aloud to a partner. Use the reduced form *YOU-sta*.

1. When I was younger, I used to _____.
2. As a child, I used to want money for _____.
3. In my country, people used to _____.
4. Before the Internet was invented, people used to _____.
5. In my last English class, we used to _____.

# Communication

**A.** Look at the artifacts from the Jamestown Colony. Imagine at least six things these colonists did every day. Use *used to*, *would*, or the simple past tense.

They probably **used to** cook food every day.

That means they **made** fires every day too.

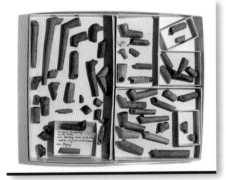
▲ Artifacts from the Jamestown Colony tell us about the colonists' everyday lives.

**B.** Think of at least six things you do every day that the colonists didn't do. Use *didn't use to* or the simple past tense.

They **didn't use to** go to school every day.

And they **didn't do** any homework either.

 **Goal 2** | **Talk about your grandparents' daily lives**

Work with a partner. Discuss the most important differences between your life and your grandparent's lives. Talk about transportation, entertainment, and doing household chores.

## Language Expansion: Separable phrasal verbs

> **give up**   **bring up**   **help out**   **switch on**   **keep away**   **put on**

**A.** Fill in the blank with the phrasal verb from the box that is closest in meaning to the verb in parentheses. Use the correct form of the verb. Use your dictionary to help you.

Hi, my name is Susie, and I live in the Nunavut Territory in Canada. Here in Nunavut, life hasn't changed as much as it has in other places. It's true—nowadays, we can _____ (start) the furnace when it gets cold, and we use modern rifles to _____ (repel) the polar bears, but we haven't _____ (relinquish) other things. We _____ (raise) our children in the land our people have lived in for thousands of years. We teach them to _____ (don) our traditional clothing to stay warm in the winter, and we teach them to always _____ (aid) their family and their community. Those things will never change.

**B.** Work with a partner to complete the sentences.

1. I hope I never have to give _____ up.
2. When I get home, I usually switch _____ on.
3. Parents work hard to bring _____ up.
4. I always try to help _____ out.
5. When I get dressed, I never forget to put _____ on.

## Grammar: Past passive voice

▲ An Inuit man builds an igloo.

| **Active voice** | **Passive voice** |
|---|---|
| Subject + transitive verb + direct object | Direct object + *was/were* + past participle of transitive verb |
| Inuit people **built** igloos from blocks of ice.<br>My grandmother **made** the family's clothes. | Igloos **were built** from blocks of ice (by Inuit people).<br>The family's clothes **were made** by my grandmother. |

*We use the passive voice with transitive verbs when the focus is on the object.
*The passive in the past tense is formed with the simple past form of *be* plus the past participle of the main verb.
*Sometimes we use a *by* phrase with the passive.

**A.** Complete each sentence with the past passive form of the verb in parentheses.

1. Money for voyages to the New World _____ (provide) by investors.
2. Glass beads _____ (trade) for food.
3. Pipes _____ (use) for smoking tobacco.
4. Wild animals _____ (hunt) by Native Americans.
5. Chocolate _____ (drink) by the Aztecs.

 **B.** How did things get done in the past in your country? Complete each sentence with the past passive form of the verb in parentheses and your own ideas.

1. Most of the time, meals _____ (prepare) by _____.
2. In general, a family's income _____ (earn) by _____.
3. Clothes _____ (make) by _____.
4. People _____ (tell) about important news by _____.
5. Many children _____ (teach) by _____.

## Conversation

**A.** Listen to the conversation. What was life like for Carl's grandparents?

Track 2-17

**Louise:** Hi, Carl. Can I ask you a serious question?
**Carl:** Sure. Go ahead.
**Louise:** Do you think your life will be very different from your grandparents' lives?
**Carl:** Maybe. Back then, important decisions were always made by the husband. And today, women . . .
**Louise:** What? We have our own opinions?
**Carl:** Exactly, but that's OK with me.
**Louise:** What else do you think will be different?
**Carl:** Well, all of the housework used to be done by women, and I don't mind doing some of the housework.
**Louise:** You're going to make someone very happy one day!

**B.** Practice the conversation. Switch roles and practice it again. Then make new conversations using your own ideas to answer Louise's questions.

**✓ Goal 3**    **Compare past and present ways of getting things done**

Talk to a partner. How were things done before the following services were developed, and how are they done now?

**postal service**      **city water systems**      **garbage collection service**

## Reading

 **A.** Discuss this question with a partner. Which of these were brought to the Americas by European explorers and colonists?
- horses
- peanuts
- tomatoes
- malaria
- cattle
- tobacco

**B.** Write answers to the questions.

1. In your own words, what was the Columbian Exchange? _____
   _____
   _____

2. What's one thing that wasn't in your country before the Columbian Exchange? _____
   _____
   _____

3. Why were the Native Americans in Tsenacomoco called Powhatan Indians? _____
   _____
   _____

4. Why did the colonists sometimes find empty farm fields near the Jamestown Colony? _____
   _____
   _____

5. Why were the Old World animals a problem for the Powhatan Indians?
   _____
   _____

6. Why do you think the Old World diseases were especially deadly for Native Americans? _____
   _____
   _____

The New World

# The Columbian Exchange

When European explorer Christopher Columbus landed on the island he named San Salvador in 1492, he began a process known as the Columbian Exchange. Columbus was followed by explorers, soldiers, and colonists from Spain, Portugal, the Netherlands, France, and England. The Europeans brought with them a great number of plants, animals, and diseases that the New World had never seen. And soon, countries in the Old World smoked American tobacco and tasted corn, tomatoes, peanuts, chili peppers, and potatoes for the first time.

The first European settlement in what is now the United States began on May 14, 1608, when an English ship landed on Jamestown Island in the present-day state of Virginia. The Jamestown Colony was founded in the middle of an Indian empire called Tsenacomoco, an area of about 8,000 square miles with more than 14,000 people. The principal Indian chief was Powhatan, father of the legendary Pocahontas, and the settlers called the native people Powhatan Indians.

Before the arrival of the English, the Powhatan Indians used to grow corn, hunt wild animals such as deer, and gather wild plants for food. When a cornfield started to produce less corn, the Indians would plant in another area. The Jamestown colonists saw these empty fields as a perfect place to grow tobacco, a New World plant that the Spanish discovered in the Caribbean. Tobacco from Virginia could be shipped to Europe and sold, and the colony's investors in England were eager to make a profit.

The Jamestown colonists also introduced several kinds of domestic animals to the New World, including cattle, horses, and chickens. The Indians had no large domestic animals, and so they had no fences around their cornfields. They were soon competing with the colonists' animals for both crops and wild food. The corn that the Indians stored for the winter months, meanwhile, became a favorite food for an animal the English brought accidentally in their ships—black rats.

In addition to the rats, colonists carried diseases from the Old World that Native Americans had never been exposed to. Diseases such as malaria, smallpox, measles, and cholera were not always deadly to Europeans, but killed a large percentage of native people in the Americas. The Columbian Exchange, therefore, came at a very high cost, but without a doubt, it was one of the most significant events in modern human history.

 **C.** Discuss this question with a partner. In the following lines from the article, what is the relationship between the noun phrases on each side of the comma (,) or dash (—)?

1. Powhatan, father of the legendary Pocahontas
2. tobacco, a New World plant
3. an animal the English brought accidentally in their ships—black rats.

## Writing

Imagine that the Columbian Exchange never happened. If you live in a New World country, the rest of the world doesn't know you exist. If you live in an Old World country, you know nothing about the Americas. Write a journal entry about a day in your life. What do you eat? What animals do you see? What do you do on a typical day?

 **Goal 4** | **Consider the impact of the Columbian Exchange**

Share your journal entry with a partner. How was your imaginary day different from a day in your real life? In your opinion, is the world better or worse because of the Columbian Exchange?

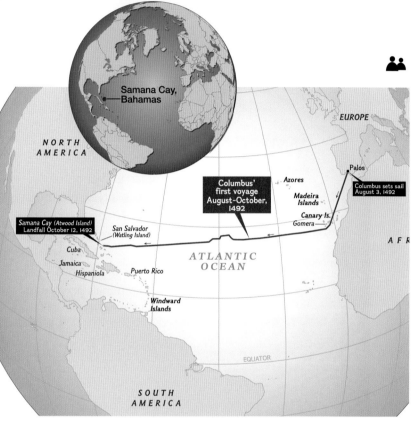

## Before You Watch

**A.** Discuss the following questions with a partner. (Don't worry if you don't know all the answers now. You can listen for the information in the video.)

1. Who was Christopher Columbus? Where is he from and why is he famous?
2. How many ships did Christopher Columbus have? Who paid for the ships?

**B.** Write each word from the box next to its definition.

| route | island | continent | voyage | spice | sailor |
|---|---|---|---|---|---|

1. _____ a long journey or trip
2. _____ one of the seven great land masses in the world
3. _____ a person who works on a ship
4. _____ a piece of land completely surrounded by water
5. _____ a pathway of travel, a way to get to a place
6. _____ a flavoring for foods, such as pepper or cinnamon

## While You Watch

**A.** Watch the video and draw lines from the people to the actions.

1. Christopher Columbus
2. King Ferdinand and Queen Isabella
3. A sailor on the Pinta
4. The Vikings

a. reached North America before Columbus.
b. shouted that he could see land.
c. paid for Columbus's voyage.
d. studied geography.

**B.** Watch the video again and fill in the blanks with the words you hear.

1. Europeans wanted _____ from India and China.
2. Columbus wanted to find a new sea _____ from Europe to Asia.
3. In 1492, Columbus persuaded King Ferdinand and Queen Isabella of Spain to give him money for the _____.
4. On October 9, after a month at sea, the _____ were very tired of looking for land.
5. Columbus and his sailors got into a small boat and went to the _____.
6. Columbus didn't know he was on a new _____. He thought he was near the coast of Asia.

## After You Watch

 How was Columbus's voyage to the New World different from a journey today? Use your imagination. Make a T-chart to show the differences.

| Columbus's voyage | Travel today |
|---|---|
|  |  |

## Communication

It's January 1492. Help Christopher Columbus prepare to talk to King Ferdinand and Queen Isabella. Make a list of things he needs for his voyage as well as a list of reasons that the king and queen should pay for those things. Then role-play the meeting.

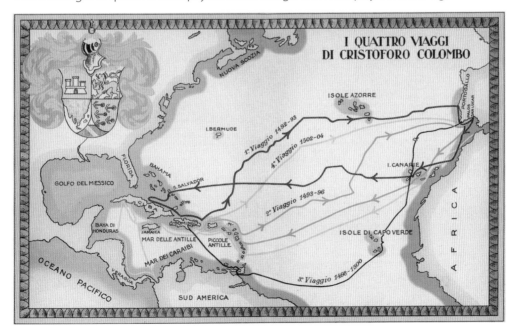

# TRAVEL

1. Where do you think these people are?
   What are they going to do?

2. Which trip would you like to take? Why?

## UNIT GOALS

Talk about preparations for a trip
Talk about different kinds of vacations
Use English at the airport
Discuss the pros and cons of tourism

## Vocabulary

**A.** Label each picture with the correct phrase.

talk to the **travel agent**

apply for a **passport**

apply for a **visa**

buy a **ticket**

make a **reservation**

check the **itinerary**

get **sightseeing** information

get a **vaccination**

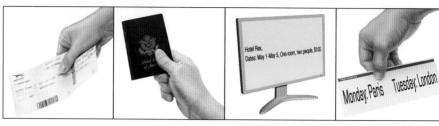

**Word Focus**

a **plane/train/hotel + reservation**

a **plane/train/bus + ticket**

**B.** What did you do before your last trip? Use vocabulary from exercise **A** and your own ideas.

## Grammar: Modals of necessity

| Modals of necessity | |
|---|---|
| **It's necessary.** | **It's not necessary.** |
| I **must** make a reservation. **have to** **'ve got to** | I **don't have to** make a reservation. |

*Must* is used in formal situations and in writing.
*Have got to* is informal.
*Have to* is used for all tenses.
*For the past, use I had to or I didn't have to.

**A.** Circle the correct modal in each sentence.

1. You (haven't to/don't have to) make reservations for the train. You can buy a ticket at the station.
2. Sorry! I can't go to the restaurant with you because (I must/I've got to) work tonight.
3. Last week, Farouk (had to/have to) take the bus to class because his car wasn't working.
4. To get a driver's license, you (must/don't have to) pass a driving test.
5. The law says that all parents (must/have got to) send their children to school.
6. Tomorrow I will (have to/must) talk to our teacher after class.

**B.** Look at the rules from the car rental company. Work with a partner to make sentences using modals of necessity.

**Car Rental Rules**

| | |
|---|---|
| have a driver's license.................... | ✓ |
| make a reservation ...................... | ✗ |
| tell the company where you're going .... | ✗ |
| be 21 years old ......................... | ✓ |
| pay with a credit card................... | ✓ |

> You have to have a driver's license.

 **C.** What are the rules in your English class? Write a list. Use *must/have to/don't have to/have got to*. Compare your list with a partner's list.

1. You **have to** hand in your homework. You **don't have to** hand in your notebook.

# Conversation

**A.** Close your book and listen to the conversation. Where is Peter going on his vacation?

Track 2-18

| Ed: | So, Peter, when are you taking your vacation? |
|---|---|
| Peter: | In September. I'm going to South Africa. |
| Ed: | Wow, South Africa! What a great trip! |
| Peter: | It will be. But first I have to get a new passport, and I have to apply for a visa. |
| Ed: | That sounds like a hassle! |
| Peter: | It's not so bad. I can get the visa from my travel agent. And I don't have to get any vaccinations. |

**B.** Practice the conversation with a partner. Switch roles and practice it again.

**C.** Look at the information. Make new conversations about these countries.

| Do travelers need . . . | a passport? | a visa? | vaccinations? | hotel reservations? |
|---|---|---|---|---|
| Turkey | Yes | Yes (online) | No | No (there are lots of hotels) |
| Australia | Yes | Yes (from the embassy) | No | Yes |
| The Philippines | Yes | No | No | Yes |

 **Goal 1** **Talk about preparations for a trip**

Talk to a partner. Say where you want to go and what you need to do to prepare for the trip.

**Real Language**

A *hassle* is an informal word for problem or trouble.

▲ Istanbul Bazaar, Turkey

▲ Ayers Rock, Australia

▲ Agno River, Philippines

## Listening

**A.** Match the descriptions to the pictures. What are some good places to do these things?

| **1. Adventure vacation** | **2. Relaxing vacation** | **3. Learning vacation** |
|---|---|---|
| Try exciting sports, like mountain climbing, bicycling, and skiing. Have experiences to tell your friends about. | Go to a beautiful place to rest and relax. Sleep late, read, listen to music, and enjoy the scenery. | Learn to do something new, like art or music, or take a class in a subject that interests you. |

**B.** Listen to three people talking about their vacations. Which country are they going to?

Track 2-19

Carla: _____

Marcus: _____

Julie: _____

**C.** Listen again. Which kind of vacation will they take?

Track 2-19

Carla: _____

Marcus: _____

Julie: _____

**D.** Which of these vacations would you enjoy the most? Explain your reasons to your partner.

## Pronunciation: Reduction of *have to, has to, got to*

**A.** Listen to the pronunciation of *have to*, *has to*, and *got to*. Notice how they sound like *hafta*, *hasta*, and *gotta*.

Track 2-20

I've **got to** finish my homework.
He **has to** clean the house.
Do you **have to** work tomorrow?

**B.** Practice the sentences with a partner. Pay attention to the pronunciation of *have to*, *has to*, and *got to*.

1. Sorry, I have to leave now.
2. I've got to apply for a visa.
3. Rosa has to pack her suitcase.
4. They've got to stay after class.

5. He has to be there at six o'clock.
6. Do you have to make a reservation?
7. You've got to answer my questions.
8. Tomorrow, I have to go to the bank.

# Communication

You and a partner have won a dream vacation in a contest. You can choose from three different trips.

Adventure tour in Africa! Travel from Egypt to South Africa in a truck, and visit 20 countries. You'll see wildlife and learn about African cultures.

Live with a family in London, and take English classes at a language school with students from many countries. Every weekend, you'll take a trip to a famous place.

Stay in a beach house! Swim, relax, or just do nothing. The house has a beautiful garden with a view of the sea, and a chef will cook all of your meals.

 **A.** Talk with a partner about the three trips and choose which one you will take together.

 **B.** What do you have to do before this trip? Think of five things.

 **C.** What will you take along? List 15 things.

> If we go to Africa, we'll have to get lots of vaccinations!

> I'll bring a digital camera to take pictures of the animals.

 **Goal 2**   **Talk about different kinds of vacations**

Get together with another pair of students. Tell them about your plans. Explain your reasons.

## Language Expansion: At the airport

**A.** Write the numbers in the circles.

| | | | | |
|---|---|---|---|---|
| 1. departures | 3. baggage claim | 5. gate | 7. boarding pass | 9. check-in counter |
| 2. security check | 4. arrivals | 6. terminal | 8. airline agent | 10. carry-on bag |

**B.** Complete the sentences. Use the words from exercise **A**.

1. When your friends come to pick you up, you meet them at the _____ area.
2. At the _____, officers look inside your bags.
3. You can take a small _____ on the plane with you.
4. After your flight, get your bags from the _____.
5. The _____ looks at your ticket and gives you a seat.
6. When you are going somewhere, you go to the _____ area.
7. The _____ is the big building at the airport.
8. The _____ is a door where you get on the airplane.
9. Your _____ is a paper with your seat number.
10. Go to the _____ to put your bags on the plane.

**C.** Tell your partner about an experience at an airport. Use words from exercise **A**.

## Grammar: Modals of prohibition

| **Modals of prohibition** | | |
|---|---|---|
| You | **must not** | bring a knife on the plane. |
| | **can't** | |

*Must not and can't mean that something is not allowed. There is a law or rule against it.

*This meaning is different from don't have to.

You **must not** take pictures here. = pictures are not allowed

You **don't have to** take pictures here. = pictures are OK but not necessary

**A.** What do these signs mean? Write sentences with *must*, *must not*, and *can't*.

1. _____
2. _____
3. _____
4. _____
5. _____

**B.** What are some things to remember when you go to the airport? Complete the sentences. Use your own ideas.

1. You have to _____.
2. You can't _____.
3. You must _____.
4. You don't have to _____.
5. You must not _____.

## Conversation

Track 2-21

**A.** Close your book and listen to the conversation. What time will the traveler get on the plane?

| | |
|---|---|
| **Check-in agent:** | Good afternoon. Where are you flying to today? |
| **Traveler:** | To Caracas. Here's my ticket. |
| **Check-in agent:** | Thank you. Would you like a window seat or an aisle seat? |
| **Traveler:** | A window seat, please. |
| **Check-in agent:** | And do you have any bags to check? |
| **Traveler:** | Just one. And this is my carry-on bag. |
| **Check-in agent:** | OK. Here's your boarding pass. You're in seat 27A. Boarding time is ten fifteen, but you must be at the gate 15 minutes before that. |
| **Traveler:** | I have a question. Is there a restaurant after the security check? |
| **Check-in agent:** | Yes, there are two. Thank you, and enjoy your flight! |

**B.** Practice the conversation with a partner. Switch roles and practice it again.

**C.** Make new conversations with this information.

1. Kuwait City/aisle seat/two bags/15C/two thirty/a place to buy a newspaper
2. London/window seat/two bags/30E/four o'clock/a pharmacy in the airport

## ✓ Goal 3   Use English at the airport

Take turns. Pretend a partner is a foreigner at your local airport. Use the illustration on the previous page to ask and answer questions about what you have to do to board your plane.

## Reading

 **A.** Discuss the questions with a partner.

1. Which places in your country get the most tourists?
2. Do the tourists cause any problems?

**B.** Find the information in the text.

1. What did Khumbu look like 50 years ago?
   a. _____
   b. _____
2. What does much of Khumbu look like today? _____
3. What problems are caused by tourists in Khumbu?
   a. _____
   b. _____
   c. _____
   d. _____
4. What actions are people taking in Khumbu?
   a. _____
   b. _____

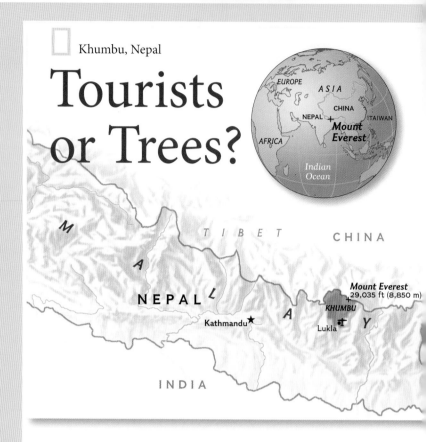

Khumbu, Nepal

# Tourists or Trees?

Around the bottom of Mount Everest, the highest mountain in the world, is a beautiful region of Nepal called Khumbu. Fifty years ago, it had thick forests, and the mountains were covered with red and pink flowers. Edmund Hillary and Tenzing Norgay started from Khumbu when they became the first people to climb Everest in 1953.

Since then, thousands of visitors have come to Khumbu to enjoy the spectacular mountain scenery and take an adventure vacation. Many tourists go trekking or hiking between villages. They sleep in very small family guesthouses.

Now everything has changed. Much of Khumbu has become a desert, in part because more than 25,000 **trekkers** pass through every year. Most sightseers arrive by small plane from Kathmandu, the capital. The planes land at the airport in Lukla. In the past, it was just a grassy field, but in 2000 a new terminal was built to allow planes and helicopters to bring in more visitors.

"We must reduce the number of tourists," says one local man. "They destroy the **trails** when they all walk in the same place. The guesthouses are crowded. People drop their water bottles and soda cans everywhere."

But the biggest problem of tourism is deforestation. Khumbu has lost most of its trees. They were cut down to build more tea houses, and to use for **firewood**. You can only see the big old trees in the wide floorboards in old houses.

"Tourists don't think about the problems they cause," says a scientist. "Especially about the wood that is used to cook their foreign food and heat water for their baths. One trekker uses as much wood in a day as five local families. They don't have to use so much wood." Now the forests have disappeared, and local people have to walk many miles to find firewood.

One possible solution is to cook and heat water with **kerosene**. But it's too expensive for many local people. "The government has got to distribute kerosene to local people," says the scientist. "It's the only way to save the forest."

People in Nepal are taking action. One group has started a program to sell cheap kerosene. The Himalayan Trust, an organization started by Edmund Hillary, has planted more than a million baby trees in Khumbu. This will save the land, and produce wood products that people can sell. In 30 years, Khumbu will have forests and flowers again.

trekkers

firewood

trail    kerosene

**C.** Match the columns to complete the reasons.

1. Tourists visit Khumbu ___
2. More tourists come to Khumbu now___
3. The forests in Khumbu are gone ___
4. Tourists use a lot of wood ___
5. People don't burn kerosene ___
6. Groups have planted baby trees ___

a. because it's too expensive.
b. because they want hot baths and foreign food.
c. because they want to start new forests.
d. because the wood was used for tourists.
e. because the mountains are beautiful.
f. because it's easy to get there.

## Communication

**A.** Talk to a partner. What can tourists do about the problems in Khumbu? Use *must, must not, have to,* and *don't have to.*

> They don't have to take a hot bath every day.

**B.** The Department of Tourism in your country has asked your group to make a report for foreign visitors in your country about how they can be good tourists. List as many ideas as you can.

**C.** Put all your ideas together. With the class, choose the three most important things.

## Writing

How can tourists help the country they visit and not hurt it? Write a paragraph about your ideas.

 **Goal 4**  **Discuss the pros and cons of tourism**

Take turns. Read your paragraphs to a small group of students. Discuss each other's opinions.

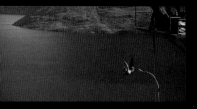

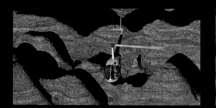

## Before You Watch

Read about the video and check the meanings of the words in **bold**.

> The city of Queenstown in New Zealand is a world center for **adventure** sports. You can ride a fast jetboat through **shallow** water, go bungee jumping off a high **bridge**, or take a helicopter **hike** in the mountains. All of these **pastimes** give travelers a **thrill**. People call Queenstown "the adventure capital of the world."

## While You Watch

 **A.** Watch the video, *Adventure Capital of the World*. Number the sports in the order that you hear about them.

helicopter hiking ＿＿＿ bungee jumping ＿＿＿ jetboating ＿＿＿

 **B.** Watch the video again and circle **T** for *true* or **F** for *false*. Then correct the false sentences.

| | | |
|---|---|---|
| 1. Queenstown is a beautiful and quiet place. | T | F |
| 2. The jetboat was invented in New Zealand. | T | F |
| 3. You can do 60 different activities in Queenstown. | T | F |
| 4. Helicopter hikers stay on top of the mountain for a long time. | T | F |
| 5. Everyone is happy after they try bungee jumping. | T | F |
| 6. People are making new adventure activities in Queenstown. | T | F |

 **C.** Watch the video again. Circle the correct answer.

1. The gap under the jump pod is (300/440) feet.
2. Jetboats were made to get around on (lakes/rivers).
3. The mountain hike takes (four/five) hours.
4. In helicopter hiking, people walk (up/down) the mountain.
5. The world's first bungee-jumping site was a (bridge/wire).

# After You Watch

Which of these activities in the video do you want to try? Why?

# Communication

**A.** Plan a three-day tour of your country for foreign visitors.

1.  What kind of tour will they have?
    adventure   history   nature   other idea: _____
2.  Which places will they visit?
3.  What will they do in each place?

**B.** Write the itinerary for your tour. Share it with another group.

# CAREERS

1. Where are the people in these pictures? What are they doing?

2. What knowledge and skills do these people have?

## UNIT GOALS

Discuss career choices
Ask and answer job-related questions
Talk about career planning
Identify career qualifications

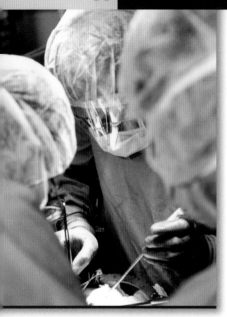

## Vocabulary

🎧 Track 2-22
**A.** Listen to a conversation between a high school senior and a career advisor. Circle each word when you hear it.

| employee | experience | owner | assistant |
|----------|-----------|-------|-----------|
| training | qualifications | volunteer | boss |

🎧 Track 2-22
**B.** Listen again. Then fill in the blanks in Ms. Carter's notes with the words in exercise **A**.

- Marcy has some work _____. She went through a _____ program to become a nurse's _____ at the hospital. It's _____ work, so Marcy doesn't get paid.
- Marcy would like to be a business _____, but she doesn't have the necessary _____ yet.
- I explained that she could start as an _____ at a business. Later, perhaps, she can be the _____ when she has her own business.

**C.** Talk to a partner. What do you think Marcy should do to prepare for her future? Did the advisor give good advice?

## Grammar: Modals for giving advice

| Modals for giving advice | |
|---|---|
| *should/shouldn't/ought to* | *had better/had better not* |
| You **should** *choose* a career that fits your personality.<br>Miguel **ought to** *become* an engineer.<br>Linda **shouldn't** *take* that office job. | You **had better** *talk* to the academic advisor before you decide on a major.<br>I **had better not** *miss* any more days of work. |

*We use modals of advice to talk about what is or isn't a good idea.
*All modals are followed by the base form of a verb.
*Had better (not) is stronger than should (not) or ought to. It means something bad could happen if the advice isn't followed.
*We can use maybe, perhaps, or I think with modals to make the advice sound gentler and friendlier.

**A.** Complete the sentences. Use your own ideas.

> **Career Advice**
> - If you want to become a successful businessperson, you should
>   _____ , but you shouldn't _____ .
> - If you really like animals, you ought to _____ .
> - When you go for a job interview, you had better _____ ,
>   and you had better not _____. Good luck!

 **B.** Read one of the problems out loud to a partner. Your partner will give you
friendly advice using *maybe*, *perhaps*, or *I think*.

1. I forgot to bring money for lunch.
2. I think I may be getting sick.
3. I want to become a doctor.
4. My job doesn't pay very well.

5. My university application was
   rejected.
6. I never remember my mother's
   birthday.

> I don't get along
> with my coworker.
>
> Maybe you
> should avoid him.

# Conversation

 Track 2-23

**A.** Close your book and listen to the conversation. Why doesn't Bob like his job?

**Miranda:** Hi Bob. How's it going?
**Bob:** Not so good. I think I need a new job.
**Miranda:** You do look stressed out. What is it you do again?
**Bob:** I'm an administrative assistant. That's like a secretary, but I have
more responsibilities.
**Miranda:** Do you have a good boss?
**Bob:** Sure. He's the owner of the company, and he's pretty nice, actually.
**Miranda:** So what's the problem? Is it the other people you work with?
**Bob:** No, my coworkers are fine, but I do the same thing every day.
**Miranda:** Maybe you should start looking for a more interesting job.
**Bob:** You're right. I can probably find something better.

 **B.** Practice the conversation with a partner. Switch roles and practice it again.

## ✓ Goal 1    Discuss career choices

Work with a partner. Choose one of the careers and describe the training, experience, and other qualifications required for that career. Then talk about the advantages and disadvantages of having that career.

| | |
|---|---|
| **sales representative** | **homemaker** |
| **lawyer** | **information technology specialist** |
| **computer software engineer** | **health care worker** |

## Listening

**A.** What makes a good job? Rank the following from 1 (most important) to 6 (least important).

\_\_\_\_\_ amount of vacation time      \_\_\_\_\_ distance from home

\_\_\_\_\_ wage or salary level      \_\_\_\_\_ long-term employment

\_\_\_\_\_ working alone or with others      \_\_\_\_\_ interesting job duties

**B.** Listen to an interview with a restaurant owner. Why did he start his own business?

Track 2-24

**C.** Listen again and answer the questions.

Track 2-24
1. When did Mr. Sangumram open the New Thailand restaurant? _____
2. Who is the cook at the restaurant? _____
3. What kind of food is served at the restaurant? _____
4. How far from the owner's home is the restaurant? _____
5. How many employees in all work at the restaurant? _____
6. What does Mr. Sangumram's wife do for a living? _____

### Engage!

Is it better to be a business owner or to be an employee?

## Pronunciation: Intonation in questions

In *yes/no* questions, the speaker's voice rises on the last content word.

**Did you finish the homework?**

**Is Mark going to talk to her?**

In questions with *wh-* words, we use a rising then falling intonation over the last content word.

**When is your birthday?**

**What was the movie about?**

Track 2-25 **A.** Listen to the following questions. Then listen again and repeat.

**_Yes/no_ questions**

1. Do you have enough money?
2. Was the car in the garage?
3. Is she your cousin?
4. Did you miss the bus?
5. Are you going downtown with us?

**_Wh-_ questions**

6. Why is he shouting?
7. How old are you?
8. Which one should I take?
9. What's the matter?
10. How many inches are in a foot?

 **B.** Write new questions. Then take turns with a partner asking and answering the questions.

| _Yes/no_ questions | _Wh-_ questions |
|---|---|
| 1.  Is that a good book? | 6.  Where's my backpack? |
| 2.  Do you have any coffee? | 7.  When are we leaving? |
| 3.  _____ | 8.  _____ |
| 4.  _____ | 9.  _____ |
| 5.  _____ | 10. _____ |

## Communication

 **A.** Imagine that Mr. Sangumram needs a new employee at the New Thailand restaurant. Choose one of the following jobs and imagine the questions that Mr. Sangumram might ask a job applicant. Then role-play the job interview for the class.

**assistant cook**

**dishwasher**

**waiter**

Is vacation time important to you?

Not really. I'd rather work more and make more money.

✓ **Goal 2**  **Ask and answer job-related questions**

Imagine you are a career advisor. Ask a partner questions to find out about his or her interests and work experience. Then recommend a career.

▲ A. J. Coston,
   volunteer firefighter

# Language Expansion: Participial adjectives

**A.** Read the article about A. J. Coston. What nouns do the words in blue describe?

A. J. Coston isn't waiting to start his dream job. At age 18, he's a weekend volunteer firefighter in the United States. During the week, he lives at home with his mom, dad, and sister, and does his main job: going to high school. "I always wanted to get into firefighting since I was a little kid watching fire trucks go by," he says. "One day I was **bored** and on the Internet, and I found out that Loudoun County offered a junior firefighter program."

Some of A. J.'s friends are **surprised** by his decision to spend weekends at the firehouse, but to A. J., helping people is more **satisfying** than anything else. The job is never **boring**, either, since firefighters get called to all sorts of emergencies. He recounts one **terrifying** 911 call after four children were struck by lightning.

A. J. will be off to college next fall, and plans to study what he's most **interested** in: emergency medical care. "I want to be a flight medic on a helicopter eventually," he says.

**B.** A noun described by an *–ed* participial adjective experiences something. Complete the sentences so they are true for you.

1. I am **bored** by _____.
2. Last week, I was **surprised** by _____.
3. I am always **pleased** by _____.

**C.** A noun described by an *–ing* participial adjective causes you to experience something. Complete the sentences so they are true for you.

1. For me, _____ is very **satisfying**.
2. I don't like _____ because it's **boring**.
3. I think _____ is absolutely **terrifying**.

# Grammar: Indefinite pronouns

| **Indefinite pronouns** | | | | | |
| --- | --- | --- | --- | --- | --- |
| ***-one*** | | ***-body*** | | ***-thing*** | |
| someone | everyone | somebody | everybody | something | everything |
| anyone | no one | anybody | nobody | anything | nothing |

**Everyone** in the audience *was* laughing.
I'm going even if **nobody** *wants* to go with me.
**Something** *is* bothering her, but I don't know what it is.

*We use indefinite pronouns to talk about unknown or indefinite people or things.
*Singular verbs are used with all indefinite pronouns.
*The indefinite pronouns that end in *-one* and *-body* refer to people.
*All indefinite pronouns except for *no one* are written as one word.

**A.** Complete the sentences with the simple present form of the verb in parentheses.

1. Everybody in my family _____ (enjoy) eating ice cream.
2. The university is looking for someone who _____ (plan) to study nanotechnology.
3. Nothing _____ (be) more discouraging than doing a job you don't like.
4. Nobody really _____ (know) what will happen in the future.

 **B.** Take turns reading the situation to a partner. Discuss the choices and circle the correct word.

1. *There are 18 students in the class. One student wants to leave early.* (Somebody/ Everybody) wants to leave early.
2. *You have never heard of the field of ethnobotany before.* I don't know (anything/ something) about ethnobotany.
3. *None of your friends, acquaintances, or family members have a luxury car.* (Anyone/No one) I know has a luxury car.
4. *You want to learn to speak Japanese. You are looking for a tutor.* I need to find (somebody/everybody) who speaks Japanese.

## Conversation

**A.** Listen to the conversation. What is the man planning to do?

Track 2-26

| | |
|---|---|
| **Parker:** | What do you want to do when you finish school? |
| **Kimberly:** | I'm not sure, but I want to do something interesting. |
| **Parker:** | Of course! Everybody wants that, but you need to start planning. |
| **Kimberly:** | OK, what are you planning to do when you finish school? |
| **Parker:** | I'm planning to enroll in a training program. They teach you how to install custom car stereos. |
| **Kimberly:** | You sound excited about that. |
| **Parker:** | I am! You know I've always loved cars, and the program is only four months long, so I can get a job really soon. |
| **Kimberly:** | That sounds great! I need to start thinking about my future, too. |
| **Parker:** | Mmm hmm. That's what I said before. |
| **Kimberly:** | And you're right, as usual. |

 **B.** Practice the conversation with a partner. Switch roles and practice it again. Make a new conversation using your own plans for the future.

 **Goal 3** | **Talk about career planning**

Talk to a partner. What kind of career would be interesting and satisfying to you? What are you doing now to prepare for your future career?

## Reading

 **A.** Discuss your answers with a partner. What's your opinion?
- What's the biggest threat to the earth's rainforests?
- What's the best way to deal with that threat?

**B.** Discuss these questions with a partner.

1. In the Ecuadoran rainforest, who is using the rainforest plants?
2. What do ethnobotanists study?
3. In the third paragraph, which of the two methods for collecting plants is sustainable?
4. What does Fadiman's data show about the Ecuadoran rainforest?
5. How do you think other people might use Fadiman's data?
6. Why are the people who live in the rainforest excited about talking to Fadiman?

**C.** Word parts sometimes help us understand the meaning of a new word. Circle the parts of the following words and write a brief definition for each one.

1. overhead  high over your head
2. underfoot_____
3. waterproof _____
4. non-sustainable _____
5. geosciences _____
6. fieldwork _____

---

**Word Focus**

**mishmash** = a combination of things that can't be distinguished
**flora** = plant species
**fauna** = animal species
**sustainable** = describes the use of natural resources at a steady level that is not likely to harm the environment

---

☐ Ecuador

Deep in an Ecuadoran rainforest, monkeys overhead and poisonous snakes underfoot, Dr. Maria Fadiman goes to work. "It looks like one big, green **mishmash** to me, but the people who live here can single out the right plants for medicine, or the one to eat if you cut out the little part in the very center. Each house is made entirely from the forest— the poles that hold it up, the floors, the thatch on the walls, the vines that tie it, the palm leaf sleeping mats, the baskets, everything. It's strong, it's waterproof, it works, and it's all done in a way that's in balance with nature."

That balance is at the center of Fadiman's research. As an ethnobotanist, she studies how people interact with plants. "Looking at conservation without including people in the equation is a fantasy," she says. "So the focus of my work is finding a balance where people use resources in a sustainable way that allows **flora** and **fauna** to remain intact."

At her field site in Ecuador, Fadiman studies **sustainable** and non-sustainable methods used to collect fiber plants and palms. Collecting plants for fiber can involve cutting down entire trees or just the specific parts of plants that will be used. Fadiman's data reveals where and why such differences exist in Ecuador's rainforests. In many cases, no written record of plant knowledge exists. Recognizing this, Fadiman's first effort is to record all the information that local people can provide.

In the field, Fadiman eats, sleeps, works, and collects native plants with local families. "When I come all this way because I think their information is important, it generates local excitement. Suddenly plant knowledge is valued." Whether sitting around a cook fire, walking through mud to brush her teeth in the river, or trying to do some basket weaving, she treasures both the information and experiences she gathers.

An assistant professor in the Department of Geosciences at Florida Atlantic University, she says, "I want to make fieldwork real to my students. If they can picture the little girl who always comes to the river with me instead of a statistic, it will mean much more. I hope my work will change even a small part of the general consciousness."

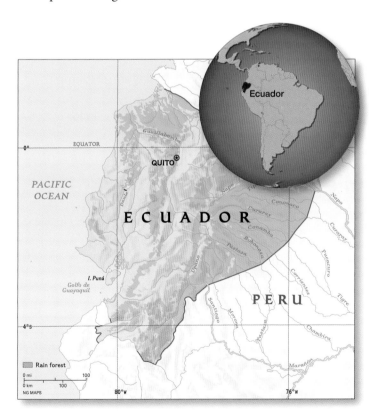

## Communication

Discuss your answers to these questions with a partner.

- What do you think Dr. Maria Fadiman did to prepare for her career as an ethnobotanist?
- Based on the article, what makes Dr. Fadiman a good ethnobotanist?

## Writing

Think about one of your dream jobs. Then fill out the questionnaire.

### Dream Job Questionnaire

1. What is your dream job? _____
2. What specific education would someone need for this job? _____
   _____
3. What life experiences might be helpful to have for this job? _____
   _____
   _____
4. What personal qualities would make someone good at this job? _____
   _____
   _____
5. Are you qualified for this job? (If not, how could you become qualified?)
   _____
   _____
   _____
   _____

 **Goal 4** | **Identify career qualifications**

Talk to a partner about the information on your questionnaire. Discuss the qualifications for your dream job and whether you are qualified for that job.

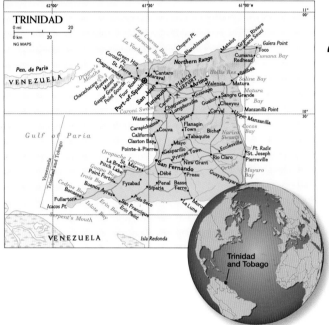

# Before You Watch

**A.** What do you know about the islands of Trinidad and Tobago? Circle the correct answer.

1. The climate of Trinidad and Tobago is (cool/tropical).
2. The topography of Trinidad and Tobago is (somewhat mountainous/completely flat).
3. The principal language of Trinidad and Tobago is (Spanish/English).

**B.** Complete the sentences with a word from the box.

| wildlife   hummingbird   paradise   nest   ornithologist |
|---|

1. A _____ is a very tiny bird.
2. An _____ studies birds.
3. _____ is a place where everything is beautiful, delightful, and peaceful.
4. Panda bears, honeybees, and dolphins are all examples of _____.
5. A _____ is a home that birds build for themselves.

▲ The scarlet ibis is the national bird of Trinidad and Tobago.

# While You Watch

**A.** Watch the video, *Trinidad Bird Man*. Check (✓) Roger Neckles's job qualifications.

☐ He enjoys being outdoors.

☐ He can take photographs.

☐ He doesn't mind working for a low salary.

☐ He's very patient.

☐ He's knowledgeable and enthusiastic about birds.

☐ He's an excellent writer.

**B.** Watch the video again. Fill in the blanks with the word or words you hear.

1. "This is the best time of the day for me, getting up at _____ in the morning."
2. It seems Neckles really has found his own _____.
3. There are about _____ different types of birds on the island, and Neckles is trying to photograph them all.
4. He's been trying to photograph this hummingbird for _____ weeks. It's been a very long wait.
5. "I have no plans to give this up at all because I figure I could do this for _____. Every time I go out I see something new."

▲ Roger Neckles

## After You Watch

**A.** Interview a partner and write down his or her answers.

1. What time do you like to get up in the morning? _____
2. How do you feel about spending a lot of time outdoors? _____
3. Are you a very patient person? Why or why not? _____
   _____
4. Do you prefer to wear casual clothes or stylish clothes? _____
5. What do you think is the most interesting kind of wildlife? _____

**B.** Should your partner become a wildlife photographer? Tell the class why or why not.

## Communication

1. Brainstorm the names of 15 occupations and write each one on a small piece of paper. Mix up the papers and put them face-down in a stack.
2. Start with one classmate in your group. Take three of the pieces of paper, but don't let your classmate see them. Ask questions about his or her qualifications, likes, and dislikes.
3. Decide which of the three occupations would be best for your classmate.

> You should become a _____ because . . .

# CELEBRATIONS

1. Which of these things do you find in each photo?
   a. costumes
   b. parade
   c. fireworks
   d. float(s)

2. What is your favorite celebration?

3. What do people do there?

## UNIT GOALS

Describe a festival
Compare holidays in different countries
Talk about personal celebrations
Share holiday traditions

# UNIT 12

▲ Men in traditional Scottish costumes take part in Hogmanay celebrations.

## Vocabulary

**A.** Read about a special New Year's celebration.

New Year's Day is a **holiday** around the world, but people in Edinburgh, Scotland, **celebrate** it in an **exciting** way. They have a **festival** called Hogmanay. Hogmanay **takes place** all around the city, from December 29 to January 1. It starts with a parade on the night of December 29. On New Year's Eve, there is a street party with fireworks, and people wear very **colorful** costumes. There is always a big **crowd** even though it's very cold. One year, more than 100,000 people **participated**. The celebration in Edinburgh is very **well-known**, but the **annual** Hogmanay festivals in other cities in Scotland are popular too.

**B.** Write the words in **blue** next to the correct meanings.

1. every year _____
2. happen _____
3. famous _____
4. a day when people don't work _____
5. very large group of people in one place _____
6. makes you feel happy and enthusiastic _____
7. with many different colors _____
8. a time with many performances of music, dance, etc. _____
9. do something enjoyable for a special day _____
10. took part in _____

 **C.** Discuss these questions with a partner.

1. What festivals have you participated in? What other festivals do you know about?
2. Would you like to participate in Hogmanay in Edinburgh? Why, or why not?

## Grammar: Comparisons with *as . . . as*

**A.** Study the sentences and circle the correct response.

**Mother's Day is as important as Father's Day.**
**The Art Fair isn't as big as the Film Festival.**

1. The first sentence talks about things that are (the same/different).
2. The second sentence talks about things that are (the same/different).

| *As . . . as* | | |
|---|---|---|
| Subject + **be** + **(not) as** + adjective + **as** + complement | | |
| New Year's is<br>Hogmanay is | **as** exciting **as**<br>**not as** popular **as** | National Day.<br>Carnival. |

*We use *as . . . as* to say that two things are the same in some way.
*We use *not as . . . as* to say that two things are different in some way.

**B.** Look at the information about the two festivals. Write sentences with *(not) as . . . as.*

|  | **The Spring Festival** | **The Harvest Fair** |
|---|---|---|
| 1. (old) | started in 1970 | started in 1970 |
| 2. (long) | 2 days | 4 days |
| 3. (popular) | 5000 people | 5000 people |
| 4. (expensive) | tickets were $5 | tickets were $20 |
| 5. (big) | 10 plays | 23 plays |
| 6. (well-known) | on a few TV shows | on many TV shows |

1.  The Spring Festival   *is as old as the Harvest Fair*                              .
2.  The Spring Festival   _____ .
3.  _____ .
4.  _____ .
5.  _____ .
6.  _____ .

 **C.** Choose two festivals or holidays. Make sentences with *as . . . as* comparing the celebrations.

> Thanksgiving is as enjoyable as New Year.

> New Year isn't as expensive as Thanksgiving.

# Conversation

Track 2-27

**A.** Close your book and listen to the conversation. When is the festival they talk about?

**Dean:** Yuki, are there any special festivals in your city?

**Yuki:** Oh, we have lots of festivals in Tokyo! My favorite is called *Setsubun*.

**Dean:** Really? What's that?

**Yuki:** Well, it takes place in February. We celebrate the last day of winter.

**Dean:** What do you do then?

**Yuki:** People throw special beans for good luck, and they say "Out with bad luck, in with good luck!" Then you eat one bean for each year of your age. And there are lots of parties.

**Dean:** That sounds like fun.

**Yuki:** It is!

 **B.** Practice the conversation with a partner. Switch roles and practice it again.

▲ a Setsubun procession

✔ **Goal 1**  **Describe a festival**

Talk to a partner about a special celebration in your city. Tell your partner when, why, and how you celebrate this festival.

## Listening

**A.** Listen to three people talk about a holiday in their country. Number the countries in the order that you hear about them.

Track 2-28

    a. Japan ____        b. Mexico ____       c. United States ____

**B.** Listen again and fill in the chart.

Track 2-28

| Halloween | Country: _____ |
| --- | --- |
| | When is it? _____ |
| | How do people celebrate it? |
| | a. put on _____ |
| | b. ask for _____ |
| | c. watch _____ |
| | What is the special food? |
| | a. _____ |
| | b. _____ |
| **Day of the Dead** | Country: _____ |
| | When is it? _____ |
| | How do people celebrate it? |
| | a. go to the cemetery with _____ |
| | b. bring _____ |
| | What is the special food? |
| | a. sweet _____ |
| | b. shaped like skulls _____ |
| **O-Bon** | Country: _____ |
| | When is it? _____ |
| | How do people celebrate it? |
| | a. go back to _____ |
| | b. participate in a special _____ |
| | c. make big _____ |

**C.** Discuss these questions with a partner.

1. Do you know about any other holidays like this?
2. Why do you think different countries have similar holidays?

## Pronunciation: Question intonation with lists

Track 2-29

**A.** Listen to the sentences. Notice how the intonation rises and falls in questions with a list of choices.

1. Would you like cake, ice cream, or fruit?

2. Is O-Bon in July or August?

Track 2-30

**B.** Read the sentences and mark the intonation with arrows. Then listen and check your answers.

1. Would you like to visit Japan, Mexico, or the United States?
2. Would you like coffee, tea, hot chocolate, or water?
3. Do you take a bath in the morning or at night?
4. Would you rather have a cat, a dog, or a bird?
5. Do you want to go to a party or stay home?

 **C.** Take turns with a partner asking and answering the questions in exercise **B.** Explain your reasons.

## Communication

 Imagine your group can take a trip to participate in one of the holidays in exercise **A** on page 138. Discuss these questions. Then explain your group's final decision to the class.

1. How are these holidays similar? Think of as many ways as you can.
2. How are they different?
3. What could visitors do at each holiday?
4. Which holiday would you like to participate in? Why?

 **Goal 2** **Compare holidays in different countries**

Take turns. Tell a partner how the different groups' trips will be similar and how they will be different.

## Language Expansion: Greetings for celebrations

**A.** Look at the greetings and write each one under the correct card.

| | |
|---|---|
| ~~Best wishes!~~ | Happy New Year! |
| Congratulations! | Happy anniversary! |

1. _Best wishes!_

2. _____

3. _____

4. _____

## Grammar: *Would rather*

**A.** Write the name under the correct picture.

**Chris:**  I don't like big parties. *I'd rather* celebrate my graduation with a few friends.

**Pat:**  I want to go on a picnic with my family for my graduation. *I'd rather not* have a party.

| *Would rather* | |
|---|---|
| Statement | I **would**/I**'d rather** go to the park on Saturday. |
| Negative | I **would rather not**/I**'d rather not** go to the meeting. |
| *Yes/no* questions | **Would** you **rather** go to lunch later? |

\*Use *would rather* + base form of the verb.
\*Use *would rather* to talk about things you prefer or like more.

**B.** Write sentences about things you like to do on your graduation with *I'd rather*.

1. have (a big party/a small party) _I'd rather have a big party._

2. eat (at home/in a restaurant) _____

3. invite (lots of people/a few close friends) _____

4. get (flowers/presents) _____

5. wear (nice clothes/jeans and a t-shirt) _____

1. _____

2. _____

**C.** Write questions with *would rather*. Then ask a partner.

1. eat at home/go to a restaurant
   *Would you rather eat at home or go to a restaurant?*

2. send a greetings card/make a phone call

   _____

3. watch TV/read a book

   _____

4. go to a basketball game/(your own idea)

   _____

5. (your own idea)/(your own idea)

   _____

# Conversation

**A.** Close your book and listen to the conversation. Which celebration is coming soon?

Track 2-31

| | |
|---|---|
| **Mike:** | New Year's Eve is next week. What would you like to do? |
| **Katie:** | Let's go out dancing! |
| **Mike:** | I'd rather just stay home and go to bed early. |
| **Katie:** | That's boring! We could go out for dinner. Or would you rather go to a movie? |
| **Mike:** | I'd rather not go out. It's always so noisy and crowded. |
| **Katie:** | I have an idea. Let's cook a nice dinner at home and invite a few friends. |
| **Mike:** | That sounds like a better plan. |

**B.** Practice the conversation with a partner. Switch roles and practice it again.

**C.** Make notes. What do you usually do to celebrate these days?

| New Year | Your favorite holiday: _____ |
|---|---|
| | |

 **D.** Work with a partner. Make plans to celebrate one of these days together.

✓ **Goal 3**　**Talk about personal celebrations**

Join another pair of students and share your plans.

# Reading

**A.** Discuss these questions with a partner.

1. What are the most important holidays in your country?
2. Are they new or old? How did they start?

**B.** Find this information in the reading.

1. the number of people who celebrate Kwanzaa now _____
2. the dates of Kwanzaa _____
3. the year when Kwanzaa started ____
4. the person who started Kwanzaa ___
   _____
5. three countries where people celebrate Kwanzaa _____
6. the most important symbol of Kwanzaa
   _____
7. the colors of Kwanzaa _____
   _____

**C.** Circle **T** for *true*, **F** for *false*, or **NI** for *no information* (if the answer is not in the reading).

1. Kwanzaa is celebrated at the end of the year.          T   F   NI
2. Kwanzaa is a holiday for African-Americans.            T   F   NI
3. Kwanzaa is a very old holiday.                         T   F   NI
4. People in Africa celebrate Kwanzaa.                    T   F   NI
5. People spend a lot of time with their families during Kwanzaa.   T   F   NI
6. Children receive presents at the end of Kwanzaa.       T   F   NI
7. Everyone thinks Kwanzaa is an important holiday.       T   F   NI

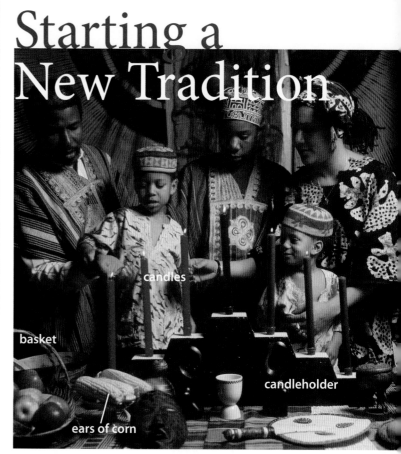

New York, United States

# Starting a New Tradition

candles

basket

candleholder

ears of corn

Shantelle Davis is a nine-year-old girl in New York. On a cold night in December, her family is standing around the kitchen table while she lights a **candle**. The table is decorated with **baskets** of fruit and vegetables and **ears of corn** for Shantelle and her two brothers.

"This candle represents *umoja*, an African word that means being together," Shantelle says. "That's the most important thing for a family."

Tonight is the first night of Kwanzaa, and Shantelle is spending the holiday with her family. More than 5 million African-Americans celebrate Kwanzaa every year from December 26 until January 1. It's a time when they get together with their families to think about their history and their ancestors in Africa.

Kwanzaa is very unusual because it was started by one man. In 1966, an American named Maulana Karenga wanted a holiday for African-Americans to honor their culture and traditions. So he used words and customs from Africa to create a new celebration. He took the name Kwanzaa from the words for "first fruits" in Swahili, an African language. At first, a few American families had small celebrations at home. Now, there are also Kwanzaa events in schools and public places, and Kwanzaa has spread to other countries like Canada and Jamaica.

The main symbol of Kwanzaa is a **candleholder** with seven candles, one for each of the principles of Kwanzaa. Each night, a family member lights one of the candles and talks about the idea it represents: being together, being yourself, helping each other, sharing, having a goal, creating, and believing. The candles are red, black, and green, the colors of Kwanzaa. The parents also pour drinks to honor family members who have died. On the last night of Kwanzaa, there is a big dinner with African food, and children receive small presents.

Today people can buy Kwanzaa greeting cards and special Kwanzaa clothes. Stores sell Kwanzaa candles and candleholders. Some people don't believe that Kwanzaa is

a real holiday, because it's so new. But other people say that customs and celebrations are always changing and that Kwanzaa shows what is important in people's lives.

Shantelle Davis says she likes Kwanzaa because it's fun. "But I also learn new things every year," she says.

# Communication

**A.** Circle your opinion about these sentences.

1. A new holiday isn't a real holiday.
   a. I agree.   b. I'm not sure.   c. I disagree.

2. Some old holidays are boring and not very important now.
   a. I agree.   b. I'm not sure.   c. I disagree.

3. Our country should start a new holiday.
   a. I agree.   b. I'm not sure.   c. I disagree.

4. People spend too much money for holidays.
   a. I agree.   b. I'm not sure.   c. I disagree.

5. It's very important to keep all of the old holiday customs.
   a. I agree.   b. I'm not sure.   c. I disagree.

 **B.** Compare your opinions with the opinions of other students. Talk about things your family does to celebrate holidays.

# Writing

Choose one of the statements from exercise **A** and write a paragraph about your opinion. Be sure to give examples and explanations.

 **Goal 4**  **Share holiday traditions**

Read your paragraph to a partner or to the class.

Mongolia

RUSSIA

Ulaanbaatar
(Ulan Bator)

MONGOLIA

| 0 mi | 600 |

| 0 km | 600 |

NG MAPS

BEIJING
(PEKING) ⊗

CHINA

## Before You Watch

Discuss these questions with a partner.

1. What do you know about Mongolia?
2. Have you ever seen a horse race? Describe what you saw.

## While You Watch

**A.** Watch the video, *Young Riders of Mongolia*. Write two unusual things about the Naadam horse race.

1. _____
2. _____

**B.** Watch the video again. Circle **T** for *true* or **F** for *false*.

1. In Mongolia today, people ride horses only for
   special celebrations.                                T    F
2. The Naadam Festival celebrates traditional sports.   T    F
3. The Naadam horse race is very short.                 T    F
4. People want to get close to the horses for
   good luck.                                           T    F
5. The winning horses get a lot of money.               T    F

▲ young Mongolian riders

 **C.** Watch the video again. Write the numbers.

1. Almost _____ years ago, Mongolia became a very large and important country.
2. All of the riders in the race are younger than _____ years old!
3. It's a big race—about _____ riders will participate in it.
4. The riders must walk the horses over _____ miles to the starting point.
5. These first riders have already been running for nearly _____ minutes!
6. The first _____ horses that finish the race get a blue sash for winning.

## After You Watch

Discuss these questions in a small group.

1. What are some traditional sports in your country?
2. Are they still popular?

## Communication

**A.** Create a festival to introduce foreigners to the culture of your country.

- Give the festival a name.
- Think of three sports, three foods, and three shows that will be in your festival.
- Make a poster to advertise your festival.

**B.** When you're finished, present your festival poster to the class.

▲ cheese rolling in England

# GLOSSARY

## Unit 1 Food from the Earth

**climate:** normal weather patterns

**coastal:** describes an area near the ocean

**crop:** a kind of plant grown for food

**farmer:** person who produces food

**flat:** describes an area without mountains

**geography:** the study of the surface of the earth

**grassland:** grassy area

**humid:** describes air that is moist

**meals:** breakfast, lunch, and dinner

**mountainous:** describes an area with mountains

**region:** a large area

**staple food:** very important food
- **grains:** corn    wheat    rice    oats    millet
- **legumes:** soybeans    lentils
- **roots:** potatoes    yams    yucca

## Unit 2 Communication

**connect:** bring together

**culture:** people with the same language and way of living

**custom:** an activity that is usual in a country

**eye contact:** a look directly at the eyes of another person

**formal:** very serious and important

**gesture:** a body movement to show something (a feeling, an idea, etc.)

**greeting:** the first words or actions used upon meeting someone

**informal:** friendly and relaxed

**rule:** the correct way to do something

**small talk:** conversation about things that aren't important

**smile:** turn one's lips up at the corners, usually to show good feelings

**traditional:** the same for a long time without changing

## Unit 3 Cities

**commute:** travel to your job

**crowded:** too full

**downtown:** the center of a city

**east:** the direction where the sun comes up—usually at the right of a map

**factory:** a place where workers make things

**freeway:** a road where cars go fast

**key:** (on a map) the section of a map that explains the meaning of the symbols

**market:** a place where people buy and sell things outdoors

**neighborhood:** one area in a city

**noisy:** too loud

**north:** the direction that's usually at the top of a map

**population:** the number of people who live in a place

**public transportation:** trains, buses, and subways

**rural:** in the country

**scale:** (on a map) the section of a map that explains the distances

**skyscraper:** a very tall office building

**south:** the direction that's usually at the bottom of a map

**suburb:** a town outside of a city

**symbol:** a picture that represents another thing

**traffic:** cars moving on a street

**urban:** in the city

**west:** the direction where the sun goes down—usually at the left of a map

## Unit 4 The Body

**acne:** a skin condition of red spots, especially on the face

**artery:** one of the large blood vessels going from the heart

**bone:** a hard, white part of the body that makes up its frame (the skeleton)

**brain:** the organ in the head used for thinking and feeling

**dandruff:** dry skin that forms on the head and drops in little white pieces

**headache:** a pain in your head

**heart:** the organ in the chest that pumps blood through the body

**hiccup:** a sharp sound you make in your throat

**indigestion:** pain in the stomach because of something you have eaten

**insomnia:** not able to sleep

**large intestine:** the lower part of the tube in the body that carries food away from the stomach

**liver:** the organ in the body that helps in making sugar for energy and in cleaning the blood

**lung:** one of two breathing organs in the chest that supply oxygen to the blood

**muscle:** a part of the body that connects the bones and makes the body move

**nausea:** a feeling like you are going to vomit

**skin:** the outer covering of the body

**small intestine:** the upper part of the tube in the body that carries food away from the stomach

**sore throat:** a general feeling of pain in the throat

**stomach:** the internal body part where food goes after being swallowed

**vein:** any of the tubes that bring blood to the heart and lungs

## Unit 5 Challenges

**achieve:** succeed in making something happen

**adventure:** do something unusual and exciting

**amazing:** very surprising and wonderful

**challenge:** something that is new and difficult to do

**climb:** go up

**cross:** go from one side of something to the other side

**equipment:** things you need for a particular purpose

**extreme:** very great

**give up:** stop trying

**goal:** something you hope to be able to do through your efforts over time

**grow up:** grow from a child to an adult

**keep on:** continue trying

**put up with:** accept something bad without being upset

**run out of:** finish the amount of something that you have

**set out:** leave on a trip

**skill:** an activity that needs special knowledge and practice

**watch out:** be very careful

## Unit 6 Transitions

**adolescence:** the part of life when you are becoming an adult

**adult:** a person aged 20 or over

**adulthood:** the part of life when you are an adult

**baby:** a person aged 0–1

**child:** a person aged 2–12

**childhood:** the part of life when you are a child

**childish:** describes a person who is older, but acting like a child (bad)

**elderly:** describes a person who looks and acts old

**get married:** become husband and wife

**graduate:** complete your studies at a school

**have a child:** give birth to a baby

**in his/her twenties:** describes a person who is between 20 and 29 (also **in his teens, thirties, forties,** etc.)

**infancy:** the part of life when you are a baby

**mature:** describes a person who is old enough to be responsible and make good decisions

**middle-aged:** describes a person who is not young or old (about 40–60)

**move:** go to live in a different place

**old age:** the part of life when you are old

**retired:** describes a person who has stopped working in old age

**senior citizen:** an old person (polite term)

**teenager:** a person aged 13–19

**youthful:** describes a person who is older, but with the energy of a young person (good)

## Unit 7 Luxuries

**dug** (past participle of *dig*): make a hole or opening by taking away earth

**export:** sell to other countries

**flown** (past participle of *fly*): transport by plane

**fur coat:** a coat made from the hairy skin of an animal

**import:** buy from other countries

**jewelry:** decorative items that people wear such as rings, bracelets, and necklaces

**luxury:** great comfort at great expense

**meant** (past participle of *mean*): have a purpose, intend to say

**necessity:** a basic need or requirement in order to live

**pearls:** smooth, round, white objects formed naturally in oysters

**precious metals:** extremely valuable, costly metals such as gold

**precious stones:** extremely valuable, costly stones such as diamonds

**silk:** the material made by silkworms

**spread** (past participle of *spread*): cover a surface by pushing something all over it

**spun** (past participle of *spin*): twist wool, cotton, etc. into thread

**stolen** (past participle of *steal*): take something that belongs to someone else without permission

## Unit 8 Nature

**badly:** the adverb form of *bad*

**beautifully:** the adverb form of *beautiful*

**crocodile:** a large lizard that kills and eats other animals

**endangered:** in danger of all dying

**extinct:** doesn't exist any more, all dead

**fast:** the adverb form of *fast*

**habitat:** the place where an animal usually lives

**hunt:** to look for animals and kill them

**loudly:** the adverb form of *loud*

**predator:** an animal that kills other animals

**prey:** an animal that other animals kill to eat

**protect:** to keep safe from danger

**shark:** a large fish with sharp teeth that kills and eats fish and animals

**slowly:** the adverb form of *slow*

**species:** a kind of animal

**tame:** trained to live with people

**tiger:** a large wild cat with black stripes

**well:** the adverb form of *good*

**wild:** in nature, not controlled by people

**wildlife:** animals and plants that live in nature

**wolf:** a wild animal that's similar to a dog

## Unit 9 Life in the Past

**bring up:** raise someone and care for until fully grown

**building:** making something by joining things together

**combs:** a flat piece of plastic, metal or wood with narrow pointed teeth on one side you use to fix your hair

**farming:** the activity of growing crops or raising animals

**give up:** stop doing or having something

**glass bead:** a small round piece of glass with a hole through it

**help out:** do something good for someone

**hairbrushes:** brushes that are used to fix your hair

**hunting:** the activity of killing wild animals for food

**keep away:** make someone or something stay far from you

**pipe:** a small tube with a bowl at one end for smoking tobacco

**put on:** (clothing) to dress

**switch on:** use a switch to turn on an electrical appliance or machine

**tools:** instruments or simple pieces of equipment that you hold in your hands to do a particular kind of work

**weapon:** a tool used to harm or kill

## Unit 10 Travel

**airline agent:** a person who works for an airline at an airport

**arrivals:** the part of an airport where travelers come in

**baggage claim:** the part of an airport where travelers get their bags back

**boarding pass:** a card that shows your seat number on an airplane

**carry-on bag:** a small bag that you can take on an airplane with you

**check-in counter:** the part of an airport where travelers show their tickets and give their bags to the airline

**departures:** the part of an airport where travelers leave

**gate:** the part of an airport where travelers get on an airplane

**itinerary:** a plan for where you will go on a trip

**passport:** an official document that you must show when you enter or leave a country

**reservation:** a place that is saved for you in a hotel, airplane, train, etc.

**security check:** the part of an airport where officers look for dangerous things in travelers' bags

**sightseeing tour:** a vacation trip to look at famous places

**terminal:** a large building at an airport

**ticket:** a printed piece of paper that says you paid for a place on a train, airplane, etc.

**travel agent:** a worker who arranges trips for other people

**vaccination:** an injection that stops you from getting a particular disease

**visa:** a stamp or paper that allows you to enter a foreign country

## Unit 11 Careers

**administrative assistant:** someone who assists in organizing and supervising an organization or institution

**assistant:** someone who helps another person do their work; a word used before job titles to indicate slightly lower rank

**bored:** a feeling of being uninterested in something

**boring:** uninteresting

**boss:** the person in charge of others

**computer software engineer:** someone who designs computer programs

**employee:** someone who works for a person, business, or government

**experience:** understanding gained through doing something

**health care worker:** someone who gives medical care

**homemaker:** someone who spends a lot of time taking care of the home and family and usually does not have another job

**information technology specialist:** an expert in the theory and practice of using computers to store and analyze information

**lawyer:** a professional who practices law

**owner:** someone with a business that belongs to him or her

**qualification:** an ability that makes someone suitable to do something

**sales representative:** someone who sells goods and services, usually outside of a store

**satisfying:** something that meets your wants or needs

**surprised:** a feeling of pleasure or shock over an unexpected event

**terrifying:** causing a strong fear in someone

**training:** a process of education, instruction

**volunteer:** someone who agrees to do something because they want to, not because they have to

## Unit 12 Celebrations

**annual:** every year

**Best wishes!:** A general greeting to wish people well

**celebrate:** do something enjoyable for a special day

**colorful:** with many different colors

**Congratulations!:** a greeting you use when someone graduates or gets a new job

**costume:** special clothes that people wear for a performance or for a holiday

**crowd:** a very large group of people in one place

**exciting:** makes you feel happy and enthusiastic

**festival:** a time with many performances of music, dance, etc.

**fireworks:** things that explode in the sky to make beautiful colors during celebrations

**float:** a display on wheels that goes in a parade

**Happy anniversary!:** a greeting you use when people celebrate being married for a certain number of years (such as 10, 25, or 50)

**Happy New Year!:** a greeting you use on New Year's Day

**holiday:** a day when people don't work

**parade:** people moving in a line in a public place to celebrate a special event

**participate:** take part in

**take place:** happen

**well-known:** famous

# SKILLS INDEX

## TEXT

**10–11** Adapted from "A Slice of History," by Susan E. Goodman: National Geographic Explorer Magazine, May 2005, **22–23** Adapted from "Connect With Anybody, Anywhere," from National Geographic *Live*, Tuesday, December 11, 2007 at 7:30 p.m., **34–35** Adapted from "Megacities:" by Erla Zwingle, National Geographic Magazine, November 2002, **46–47** Adapted from "Tiny Invaders," by Kirsten Weir: National Geographic Explorer Public Website, November-December 2006, **54** Adapted from "Jenny Daltry, Herpetologist, Emerging Explorer," National Geographic News Public Website, **56** Adapted from "Alone Against the Sea," by Walter Roessing: National Geographic World Magazine, April 1997, **58–59** Adapted from "Arctic Dreams and Nightmares," by Marguerite del Giudice: National Geographic Magazine, January 2007, **66** Listening text Adapted from "Quest for Longevity Okinawa, Japan," National Geographic Interactive Edition, October 31, 2005, **70–71** "Coming of Age the Apache Way," by Nita Quintero: National Geographic Magazine, February 1980, **76–79** Vocabulary and Listening texts adapted from "Flower Trade," by Vivienne Walt: National Geographic Magazine, April 2001, **82–83** Adapted from "Perfume, the Essence of Illusion," by Cathy Newman: National Geographic Magazine, October 1998, **90** Text and Listening adapted from "Still Waters," by Fen Montaigne: National Geographic Magazine, April 2007, **94–95** Adapted from "Return of the Gray Wolf," by Douglas H. Chadwick: National Geographic Magazine, May 1998, **101** Adapted from "16 Indian Innovations: From Popcorn to Parkas," National Geographic News, September 21, 2004, **103** Listening text adapted from "What would you take to the New World?," by Karen E. Lange: National Geographic Magazine, May 2007, **106–107** Adapted from "America Found and Lost," by Charles C. Mann: National Geographic Magazine, May 2007, **128** Adapted from "Cool Job, Firefighter Takes the Heat," by Catherine Clarke Fox, National Geographic Kids (online), **130–131** Adapted from "Maria Fadiman – Ethnobotanist," from National Geographic in the Field (online).

## ILLUSTRATION

**vi-1:** National Geographic Maps; **8:** Keith Neely/illustrationOnLine.com; **10–11:** (l to r) Phil Howe/illustrationOnLine.com(3), Ted Hammod/illustrationOnLine.com, Phil Howe/illustrationOnLine.com, Steve McCracken; **12, 24:** National Geographic Maps; **32:** Bill Wood/illustrationOnLine.com; **34:** (l) Ralph Voltz/illustrationOnLine.com, (r) National Geographic Maps; **35, 36:** National Geographic Maps; **40:** (all) Sharon&Joel Harris/illustrationOnLine.com; **44, 54, 59:** Keith Neely/illustrationOnLine.com; **60, 66:** National Geographic Maps; **70:** Keith Neely/illustrationOnLine.com; **72:** National Geographic Maps; **76:** Keith Neely/illustrationOnLine.com; **84, 88, 90:** National Geographic Maps; **94:** Keith Neely/illustrationOnLine.com; **95, 102, 108:** National Geographic Maps; **112:** (all besides bmr) Patrick Gnan/illustrationOnLine.com; **112 (bmr), 116:** Ralph Voltz/illustrationOnLine.com; **117:** (all) Nesbitt Graphics, Inc.; **118:** National Geographic Maps; **119:** Keith Neely/illustrationOnLine.com; **120, 131, 132:** National Geographic Maps; **140:** (tl) Homsa/Shutterstock, (tr) jgroup/istockphoto, (bl) Tatjana Strelkova/Shutterstock, (br) dhanford/istockphoto; **144:** National Geographic Maps.

## PHOTO

**vi:** (t) Michael Nichols/National Geographic Image Collection, (bl) Bettmann/Corbis, (br) W. Robert Moore/National Geographic Image Collection; **1:** (tl) James Strachan/Getty Images, (tr) Gordon Wiltsie/National Geographic Image Collection, (bl) Michael Nichols/National Geographic Image Collection, (br) David Mclain/National Geographic Image Collection; **2–3:** (l to r) Robert Sisson/National Geographic Image Collection, Zhinong Xi/Minden Pictures/National Geographic Image Collection, Volkmar K. Wentzel/National Geographic Image Collection, Andrew H. Brown/National Geographic Image Collection; **4:** Jonas Tufvesson/AGE Fotostock; **5:** Leon Rafael/istockphoto; **6:** (t) Dorit Jordan Dotan/istockphoto, (b) elwynn1130/istockphoto; **7:** Zhang Bo/istockphoto **9:** PhotoDisc/Photolibrary; **12–13:** (l to r) Tim Laman/National Geographic Image Collection, eyedear/Shutterstock, Justin Guariglia/National Geographic Image Collection, Tim Laman/National Geographic Image Collection, Maria Stenzel/National Geographic Image Collection, Tim Laman/National Geographic Image Collection, Maria Stenzel/National Geographic Image Collection, Justin Guariglia/National Geographic Image Collection; **13:** (m) A.S. Zain/Shutterstock, (b) Paul Chesley/National Geographic Image Collection; **14–15:** (l to r) Bob Thomas/istockphoto, Dean Conger/National Geographic Image Collection (2), Catherine Yeulet/istockphoto; **16:** Alaska Stock Images/National Geographic Image Collection; **17:** (t) Pankaj & Insy Shah/Getty Images, (b) Stephanie Maze/National Geographic Image Collection; **18:** istockphoto; **9:** Bruce Dale/National Geographic Image Collection; **20:** Chris Ware/The Image Works; **21:** Manfred Rutz/Getty Images; **22:** (b): Holger Mette/Shutterstock; (t) William Allen/National Geographic Image Collection; **23:** (both) Anne Griffiths Belt/National Geographic Image Collection; **23–24:** (l to r) Rodney Brindamour/National Geographic Image Collection, Michael Nlichols/National Geographic Image Collection (2), Steve Pope/AP Images, Mary Schwalm/AP Images, Steve Pope/AP Images, Vincent J. Musi/National Geographic

Image Collection, Michael Nichols/National Geographic Image Collection; **25:** (m) Michael Nlichols/National Geographic Image Collection, (b) Vincent J. Musi/National Geographic Image Collection; **26–27:** (l to r) David Alan Harvey/National Geographic Image Collection, Winfield Parks/National Geographic Image Collection, Robert Madden/National Geographic Image Collection, Paul Cowan/Dreamstime; **28:** (t) Justin Guariglia/National Geographic Image Collection, (b) Jodi Cobb/National Geographic Image Collection; **29:** David Young Wolff/PhotoEdit; Amy Toensing/National Geographic Image Collection; **31:** Christopher Russell/Dreamstime; **33:** (t) Chepe Nicoli/istockphoto, (b) Ariel Skelley/AGE Fotostock; **34:** Stuart Franklin/National Geographic Image Collection; **36–37:** (l to r) Franc & Jean Shor/National Geographic Image Collection, Alexandra Boulat/National Geographic Image Collection, W. Robert Moore/National Geographic Image Collection, James L. Stanfield/National Geographic Image Collection, Jenny Barnard and Jonathan Green of www.fesrestoration.com, Thomas J. Abercrombie/National Geographic Image Collection, James L. Stanfield/National Geographic Image Collection, Alexandra Boulat/National Geographic Image Collection; **36:** (m) Jerónimo Alba/AGE Fotostock, (b) Jenny Barnard and Jonathan Green of www.fesrestoration.com; **37:** (b) Tatraholiday/Dreamstime; **38–39:** (l to r) Syracuse Newspapers/Tim Reese/The Image Works, John Burcham/National Geographic Image Collection, Richard Olenius/National Geographic Image Collection, Wojtek Buss/AGE Fotostock; **41:** Juanmonino/istockphoto; **42:** (l) Bob Daemmrich/The Image Works, (m) FoodPix/JupiterImages, (r) Michael Prince/Corbis; **43:** Monkey Business Images/Shutterstock; **44:** Photononstop/SuperStock; **45:** Vicki Reid/istockphoto; **46:** Eye of Science/Photo Researchers; **47:** (t) Manfred Kage/Peter Arnold; (b) Howard Sochurek/The Medical File/Peter Arnold; **48–49:** (l to r) Robert Clark/National Geographic Image Collection, Bernhard Lelle/Shutterstock, Sarah Leen/National Geographic Image Collection, Sebastian Kaulitzki/Shutterstock, Sebastian Kaulitzki/Shutterstock, Medical RF/Photo Researchers, Bernhard Lelle/Shutterstock, Sebastian Kaulitzki/Shutterstock;

**48:** (m) Andres Rodrigues/Dreamstime; (b) Sebastian Kaulitzki/Shutterstock; **49:** (b) Starblue/Dreamstime; **50–51:** (l to r) W.E. Garrett/National Geographic Image Collection, syagci/istockphoto, Emory Kristof/National Geographic Image Collection, Gordon Wiltsie/National Geographic Image Collection; **52:** (t) W.E. Garrett/National Geographic Image Collection, (b) syagci/istockphoto; **53:** Tim Pannell/Corbis; **54:** (top l to r) Malcolm Schuyl/Alamy, Fritz Hoffmann/National Geographic Image Collection, W. Perry Conway/Corbis, (bottom l to r) Kevin Krug/National Geographic Image Collection, Nick Norman/Getty Images, John Cancalosi/Alamy, Steve McCurry/National Geographic Image Collection; **56:** James A. Sugar/National Geographic Image Collection; **57:** (t) photos.com, (b) Stephen Matera/Aurora Photos/Corbis; **58:** (l) Joel Sartore/National Geographic Image Collection, (r) Mike Horn/National Geographic Image Collection; **60–61:** (l to r) Michael Nichols/National Geographic Image Collection (4), Randy Olson/National Geographic Image Collection, Dr. Gilbert H. Grosvenor/National Geographic Image Collection, Michael Nichols/National Geographic Image Collection (2); **60:** (bottom l to r) Beverly Joubert/National Geographic Image Collection, Volkmar K. Wentzel/National Geographic Image Collection, Michael Nichols/National Geographic Image Collection (2), Paul Nicklen/National Geographic Image Collection; **61:** (b) Michael Nichols/National Geographic Image Collection; **62–63:** (l to r) Digital Vision/SuperStock, Dennis O'Clair/Getty Images, Ken Wramton/Getty Images, Idealink Photography/Alamy; **64:** (l to r) Vivid Pixels/Shutterstock, Monkey Business Images/Dreamstime, Yuri Arcurs/Shutterstock, Pipa100/Dreamstime, Winfield Parks/National Geographic Image Collection; **65:** Monkey Business Images/Dreamstime; **66:** (both) Gianluca Colla/National Geographic Image Collection; **68:** (t): Thomas Perkins/istockphoto, (1 to 6) John Birdsall/The Image Works, Zsolt Nyulaszi/Shutterstock, Andres Rodriguez/Dreamstime, Elena Ray/Shutterstock, Yuri Arcurs/Shutterstock, Noam Armonn/Dreamstime; **69:** (l) Digital Vision/Getty Images, (r) Juan Monino/istockphoto; **70, 71:** Bill E. Hess/National Geographic Image Collection; **72–73:** (l to r) Richard Passmore/Getty Images, James

Strachan/Getty Images, Kevin O´Hara/AGE Fotostock, Reuters/Noor Khamis/Landov, Imagestate Media Partners Limited - Impact Photos/Alamy, Janet Wishnetsky/Photolibrary, James Strachan/Getty Images, Imagestate Media Partners Limited - Impact Photos/Alamy; **73:** (b) Reuters/Noor Khamis/Landov; **74–75:** (l to r) Marco Andras/AGE Fotostock, Ton Kinsbergen/Photo Researchers, Mira/Alamy, Schlegelmilch/Corbis, Andrew Lichtenstein/The Image Works; **77:** (t) Photodisc/Photolibrary, (b) **78:** Sisse Brimberg/National Geographic Image Collection (2), Alija/istockphoto, Tatiana Belova/istockphoto; **79:** Ton Kinsbergen/Photo Researchers; **80:** (t) Macduff Everton/National Geographic Image Collection, (b) chris_tack/istockphoto; **81:** Buzzshotz/Alamy; **82, 83:** Robb Kendrick/National Geographic Image Collection; **84–85:** (l to r) Paul A. Souders/Corbis (2), Raimund Franken/Peter Arnold (2), Paul A. Souders/Corbis, Tomas Pavelka/Shutterstock, Bridgeman Art Library, London/SuperStock, Don Fuchs/AGE Fotostock; **84:** (b) Bridgeman Art Library, London/SuperStock; **85:** (m) Jaime Plaza Van Roon/Auscape/The Image Works, (b) Don Fuchs/AGE Fotostock; **86–87:** (l to r) Albert Moldvay/National Geographic Image Collection, Stephen Frink/Getty Images, Michael Nichols/National Geographic Image Collection, Joel Sartore/National Geographic Image Collection; **88:** Nicholas DeVore/Getty Images; **89:** Forca/Dreamstime; **90:** (both) Brian J. Skerry/National Geographic Image Collection; **91:** Melissa Farlow/National Geographic Image Collection; **92:** (tl) Tim Laman/National Geographic Image Collection, (tr clockwise) Martin Rugner/AGE Fotostock, Brian J. Skerry/National Geographic Image Collection, Abraham Nowitz/National Geographic Image Collection, Cate Frost/Shutterstock, Purestock RF/JupiterImages, (bl) Gerry Ellis/Minden Pictures/National Geographic Image Collection; **93:** (t) JTB Photo/AGE Fotostock, (b) Image DJ/AGE Fotostock; **94:** Joel Sartore/National Geographic Image Collection; **96–97:** (l to r) Bates Littlehales/National Geographic Image Collection, Joseph H. Bailey/National Geographic Image Collection, Corbis/AGE Fotostock, sarininka/Shutterstock, slpix/shutterstock, JTB Photo/AGE Fotostock, slpix/shutterstock, sarininka/Shutterstock; **96:** (b) Joel